HURRICANES!

by

Peter R. Chaston

Chaston Scientific, Inc.

P.O. Box 758
Kearney, MO 64060
phone: 816-628-4770
fax: 816-628-9975

Books by Peter R. Chaston:

1. WEATHER MAPS - *How to Read and Interpret all the Basic Weather Charts -* SECOND EDITION *(ISBN: 0-9645172-4-8)*

2. TERROR FROM THE SKIES! *(ISBN: 0-9645172-1-3)*

3. HURRICANES! *(ISBN: 0-9645172-2-1)*

4. JOKES AND PUNS FOR GROAN-UPS *-co-authored   with JAMES T. MOORE* *(ISBN: 0-9645172-3-X)*

5. WEATHER BASICS *-co-authored   with JOSEPH J. BALSAMA* *(ISBN: 0-9645172-5-6)*

6. THUNDERSTORMS, TORNADOES AND HAIL! *(ISBN: 0-9645172-6-4)*

Second printing: 2000

COPYRIGHT   © 1996 by CHASTON SCIENTIFIC, INC.

Library of Congress Catalog Card Number: 95-96131

ISBN 0-9645172-2-1

Dedication

*This book is dedicated to
my wife, Mary, and to
my daughter, Valerie,
who are the joys of my life,
and to my second joy:
the love of weather.*

*Therefore, I also dedicate
this book to
everyone who enjoys and
is enthralled by
the vagaries of
weather.*

CHASTON SCIENTIFIC, INC.
P.O. Box 758
Kearney, MO 64060

H U R R I C A N E S !

TABLE OF CONTENTS

(continued)

THE FOLLOWING CHAPTERS, LISTED ON THE NEXT PAGE, ARE THE TECHNICAL SECTION OF THIS BOOK, AND ARE PREPARED FOR METEOROLOGISTS AND OTHERS DESIRING ADDITIONAL TECHNICAL DESCRIPTIVE MATERIAL ON TROPICAL CYCLONES.

INTRODUCTION

The hurricane is truly the most majestic storm on earth.

No other weather feature quite resembles the uniqueness of the hurricane. The outer edge of the storm is comprised of bands of squally showers and thunderstorms, and as the storm's center approaches, the solid rain shield yields winds of increasing fury. Finally, the calm or nearly calm hurricane eye passes overhead, often accompanied by mostly clear skies. Then, suddenly, the fury is unleashed again as the back side of the hurricane moves overhead, subsequently giving us gradually decreasing winds as the storm moves on.

Anyone who has ever lived through the ferocity of the full strength of a <u>major</u> hurricane can speak from experience about the storm's awesome power.

Hurricanes play a role in humanity's history and there is absolutely nothing that we can do to prevent hurricanes. Even if we did, Nature would have to create something else to transport the build-up of heat energy away from the tropics, which is the role of the hurricane.

In the colder part of the year, the temperature difference between the polar region and the tropics is much greater than in summer and early autumn when the hurricane season is underway. In the cold season, this greater temperature difference strengthens the jet-stream and also the low pressure systems ..the storms.. which transport warm air poleward and cold air away from the pole, generating some mixing of air. Nature's purpose in this process is to prevent the polar regions from getting progressively colder and the tropics from getting progressively hotter, which would result in a far different world climate from what we have now. The poles have a net loss of heat radiated into space, and the tropics have a net increase of heat energy. Therefore, low pressure systems necessarily mix the air, modifying the thermal contrasts.

In the summer and early fall, when the temperature differences between polar and tropical regions are much less, the jet-streams are weaker and it is rare to have a strong regular low pressure system. Thus, Nature forms the hurricane, which is a tropical low pressure system that does not form on a frontal system separating cold and warm air, and does not need a jet-stream above it. The hurricane typically forms in the tropics and transports some of the great build-up of heat energy, moisture and a property called momentum, which is related to the wind, away from the tropics.

Therefore, we are going to continue to have a hurricane season every year. Hurricanes are a normal aspect of the earth's climatic regime. Thus, we should know as much as possible about these storms so that we can cope with their destructive fury. This book details what we know about this horrific yet majestic storm. We hope you find it interesting and informative.

ABOUT THE AUTHOR

PETER R. ("Pete") CHASTON became fascinated with weather as a young boy. His personal affinity for the science of meteorology began when he experienced a few hurricanes while growing up along the East Coast. He was fascinated by having the eye of a tropical storm named Brenda go right over his home weather station, followed some two months later by Hurricane Donna's 100+ mph winds and driving sheets of horizontal rain. Winter snowstorms and blizzards also thrilled him, and weather grew to be Pete Chaston's main interest.

Having weather as an intense hobby eventually led to a career in meteorology. Pete started reading college texts and everything else he could find on weather through secondary school, and then served as a weather observer in the Air Force for four years, saving money for college.

Pete Chaston received his Bachelor of Science degree in Meteorology and Oceanography from New York University, and later, while a National Weather Service (weather bureau) forecaster, was selected for the weather service Fellowship to graduate school, underwhich he earned his Master of Science degree in Meteorology from the University of Wisconsin. It was at Wisconsin where he met Mary Gabrielski and they married almost two years later.

Pete Chaston served as a National Weather Service meteorologist from 1971 through 1995, afterwhich he took advantage of an early retirement option to found Chaston Scientific, Inc., under whose auspices this book is written.

In the weather service, Pete served at Binghamton, New York and at Hartford, Connecticut before transferring to the forecast office at Pittsburgh, Pennsylvania. He then was the Meteorologist-in-Charge of the National Weather Service Office at Rochester, New York and later became Technical Project Leader for the National Weather Service Training Center in Kansas City, Missouri.

Pete has written several books on meteorology, had a weekly newspaper column on weather, did television and radio weather and numerous talk shows, and is a regular lecturer and speechgiver. He played the role of a meteorologist in the movie, "Water", filmed for the PBS TV network and...for something different... even appeared in a Stephen King movie, "Sometimes They Come Back", and has a popular Kansas City radio program called "The Pete Chaston Doowop Show". He has taught at the State University of New York, the University of Missouri at Kansas City, the University of Kansas at Lawrence, Kansas, William Jewell College at Liberty, Missouri and lectured at other colleges. Pete Chaston has also worked with several grants involving training the nation's earth science teachers in meteorology, and has presented seminars to the National Science Teachers Association and various Academies of Science. He also gives training seminars on weather.

Pete was President of the Kansas City Chapter of the American Meteorological Society for two terms.

Pete Chaston has published scientific research articles in magazines and journals, including the National Weather Digest and Weatherwise. He developed a technique for forecasting heavy snow amounts that is widely used by forecasters nationwide. The technique is called "The Magic Chart" because it is straightforward and easy to use. He also pioneered new operational forecasting procedures now commonplace in contemporary meteorology. Some of the books Pete has written include "WEATHER MAPS - How to Read and Interpret all the Basic Weather Charts", "TERROR FROM THE SKIES!" and "HURRICANES!". With fellow meteorologist Dr. James Moore he co-authored a humorous book entitled, "JOKES AND PUNS FOR GROAN-UPS", and with science educator Joseph Balsama, he co-authored the compendium, "WEATHER BASICS", which is a preferred introduction to meteorology book. Thus, Pet Chaston has varied interests and derives great fun and enjoyment from all of them.

1. HURRICANES: AN HISTORICAL PERSPECTIVE

Figure 1. The weather symbol for a hurricane in the Northern Hemisphere.

Above is the symbol of the hurricane. Its appearance on a weather map, especially when this warm-core low pressure system is approaching a populated land area, strikes fear into the affected populous and creates a near-frenzy of activity and anticipation among meteorologists forecasting for the threatened area.

The symbol itself represents the tightly wound-up isobars of pressure around the nearly-calm and typically mostly clear eye in the center of the storm. In the Northern Hemisphere, the air circulation of the storm is counterclockwise. Well-developed hurricanes and typhoons are nearly symmetrical, with "feeder bands" of moisture energy sweeping into the storm, and an anticyclonic or clockwise outflow of air at the highest levels of the system.

The hurricane symbol represents all of this. It is appropriate for the special type of low pressure system known as the hurricane to have its own symbol, considering that the hurricane is the greatest storm on earth.

Figure 2. A hurricane moving in on a coastal community.
The devastating winds and flash flooding rains are accompanied by the surge of sea-water known as the "storm surge", upon which powerful waves occur.

The hurricane is a normal aspect of the earth's climate. If we were able to destroy hurricanes before they made landfall, Nature would have to generate another means to transport the net build-up of tropical energy towards cooler latitudes. Thus, the function of the hurricane is to contribute to the moderating and regulating of the earth's climate.

In one of Christopher Columbus' voyages to the New World in the 1490's, his group sailed unknowingly into a hurricane, but survived. The early Spanish explorers heard a term for this storm, "huracan", used by the Carib Indians of the West Indies. The word likely has a connection to "Huracan", a god of evil, who was feared by the ancient Tainos tribe of Central America. The Spanish explorers began using the word, which was later picked up by the British settlers, to become the word "hurricane" which we use today for these fierce storms from the tropics.

West of the International Date Line, at longitude 180° West in the mid-Pacific Ocean, and westward to eastern Asia, these storms are called typhoons. The first English-language use of this word appeared as "tuffoon" in 1699. In Mandarin Chinese, tai means great and feng means wind, thus, tai feng appears to be a word root. In Cantonese Chinese, toi fung has the same meaning.

Going back further, historically, one of the languages of India used the words touffon and tufan to describe a hurricane hitting coastal India. Touffon and tufan were first recorded in English in 1588.

The Arabic word, tufan, was brought to India by Arabs who settled there in the 11th century. Thus, the word may have been passed on from Arabic to an Indian language.

Even earlier, the Greek word typhon, meaning whirlwind, and also Typhon, a name given to the "father of the winds", was used by Arabs who borrowed many Greek words during the Middle Ages.

Thus, the word "typhoon" seems to be a coalescence of these roots.

Ironically, the word typhoon is not used for a hurricane coming out of the Indian Ocean. Such storms there are referred to as cyclones or tropical cyclones. Typhoon is used in the western Pacific and in eastern Asia.

The word "cyclone" apparently comes from the Greek "kuklon", which is the present participle of "kuklown", to rotate, which is related to "kuklos", meaning circle. However, the word "cyclone" was coined by Henry Piddington, an Englishman who was President of the Marine Courts at Calcutta, India. Cyclone, meaning "coil of a snake", was used for a storm. In meteorology, any low pressure system is referred to as a "cyclone", with the term "tropical cyclone" reserved for the unique form of storm which is the hurricane.

In Australia and vicinity, the term tropical cyclone is also used.

The term "hurricane" is used in the Atlantic Basin and in the eastern Pacific Basin.

In this book, the use of the word "hurricane" is applied to all of these tropical cyclones around the world.

All through history, hurricanes continue to play a significant role. Before the days of weather bureaus and weather warnings, hundreds of ships, loaded with cargo, have been sent to the bottom of the oceans by hurricanes and typhoons. Treasure hunters today continue to comb the Caribbean Sea and waters off the southeast United States for old ships and their precious bounties.

In 1857, one hurricane had the effect of nearly bankrupting the United States. In September of that year, the S.S. Central America was loaded with some 6000 pounds of precious metal from the California goldrush. The ship was en route from California to the East Coast. As this luxury steamship headed northward, it ran into a hurricane when the ship was some 200 miles east of Charleston, South Carolina. The storm was a major hurricane, causing the ocean to run "mountains high".

The S.S. Central America sprang a leak so huge that every man on board was put into emergency service bailing out the water. This continued for some 30 hours. The gold had to get through: the ship was returning to New York City where the banks were anxiously awaiting the arrival of the gold.

However, the hurricane won, with the steamship sinking, drowning 410. A smaller ship was able to rescue about 170 people, "women and children first". Most of the passengers tossed their bags heavy with gold into the Atlantic Ocean. Many who were not rescued hung onto scraps of floating wood before perishing.

Figure 3. The S.S. Central America, which sank in a major hurricane on September 1857 off South Carolina with some 6000 pounds of gold, nearly bankrupting our new Republic.

The historic importance of this tragedy is that the New York banks were nearly bankrupt, the nation was still relatively young, and a terrible civil war was about to ensue. Because of the sinking of the S.S. Central America by a hurricane, banks across the United States failed, leading to the great "Panic of 1857".

In September of 1989, just before major Hurricane Hugo slammed into Charleston, South Carolina causing major damage, the Columbus-America Discovery Group began retrieving some of the gold from the ocean floor, after the ship's location was discovered.

Hurricanes have played a major role in the course of history. In an article in the old magazine, American Mercury, back in September 1927, the former head of the weather bureau wrote, "I knew that many armadas in olden days had been defeated, not by the enemy, but by the weather, and that probably as many ships had been sent to the bottom of the sea by storms as had been destroyed by the fire of enemy fleets."

During the Spanish-American War of 1898, President McKinley told his Secretary of Agriculture, under whose jurisdiction was the United States Weather Bureau at that time, "...I am more afraid of a West Indian hurricane than I am of the entire Spanish Navy." Thus began the issuance of hurricane advisories and warnings in this country, although records of warnings related to hurricanes go back to 1873. The United States Weather Bureau, known since 1970 as the National Weather Service, began in 1870.

In analyzing and studying past hurricanes, it is essential to keep in mind that many tropical storms and hurricanes went undetected before 1960. If a passing ship happened to run into one, it was recorded and reported. After radio was developed, a ship encountering a hurricane would radio such information back to the mainland. Coastal weather radars were not installed until about 1957 and 1958, and the first weather satellite, called TIROS I, was not launched until 1960. Thus, for the advocacy of sheer accuracy, the hurricane climatology can be accepted as quite accurate only from 1960 to today.

The subsequent structure of this book is to discuss hurricanes that affect the United States, and then to discuss hurricanes elsewhere around the world. Then come the chapters describing these storms and their dynamics. The final chapters cover technical material on hurricanes, that would be of special interest to meteorologists.

I hope you enjoy this text on hurricanes. If you have any ideas or suggestions to enhance any subsequent editions of this book, please send them to Chaston Scientific, Inc. at the address given on page ii. Thank you.

2. HURRICANES AND THE UNITED STATES AND CANADA

a. Northeast U.S. and eastern Canada hurricanes

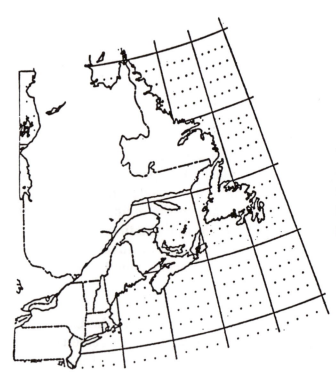

Figure 4. The northeast United States and the adjacent part of Canada are hurricane prone.

The large population centers, especially from New Jersey to the Boston area, are targets for potential disaster should a major, large and slow-moving hurricane strike this area.

For the United States, the longest period of weather records comes from the northeastern states. From the days of the Pilgrims in the 1620s to today, we can document the frequency and intensity of hurricanes striking this region.

We know that no hurricanes may affect the area for several successive years, and we know that the northeast U.S. and southeast Canada can experience several consecutive years with multiple tropical storm and hurricane strikes.

As discussed later, hurricanes intensities are rated on a scale from 1 to 5, with category 5 being the worst, with sustained winds greater than 155 miles per hour. Gusts in some of the past hurricanes have exceeded that speed, but sustained winds that high would be a rare event. For a category 5 storm to maintain such fury that far north, the storm would need to pass over warmer-than-usual ocean water on its journey northward, and may have to be moving at a swift pace as it moves away from the much warmer waters.

A critical factor of hurricanes in the U.S. northeast is that some of the largest concentrations of population reside here. From New Jersey to Maine, millions of residents live along the sea-shore. A category 5 hurricane typically has a storm surge of sea-water greater than 18 feet high, and storm surges in excess of 25 feet occur in the worst of the hurricanes. Hurricane Camille, which made landfall at Pass Christian, Mississippi, had a storm surge of 27 feet, with waves on top of it, and sustained winds of about 200 mph, which is about as extreme as a hurricane ever gets.

Category 5 hurricanes do not occur in the Atlantic basin every year. In the twentieth century, as of this writing, only TWO category 5's struck the U.S. mainland, one in Florida and Camille in Louisiana. In both cases, loss of life and catastrophic damage occurred.

Thus, although a category 5 hurricane is not common, and is even more rare to threaten the northeast, that region and southeast Canada have been struck by category 4 storms which caused widespread destruction, and there have been periods of several consecutive hurricane seasons with land-falling storms. The charts below show the notable 1953-54-55 period as an example.

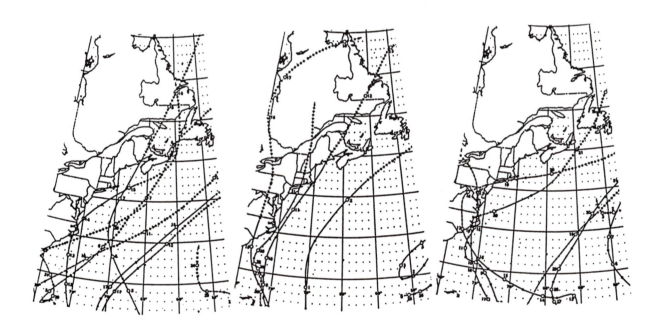

Figure 5. The northeast United States and southeast Canada are struck in three consecutive years by tropical storms and hurricanes. Paths of the storms are shown for 1953 (left), 1954 (middle), and 1955 (right).

Weather historian **DAVID LUDLUM, who founded Weatherwise magazine and who has done the most research into American weather history, wrote several books on American weather, including documentation of the past hurricanes that have hit this country.** Thanks to his meticulous and painstaking research through weather records, old diaries, old newspaper and magazine articles and other sources, we know that the northeastern United States can EXPECT to be hit by hurricanes, and occasionally can EXPECT a savage blow from a category 4 storm.

One of the earliest recorded hurricanes in the northeast affected the Pilgrims' colony at Plimouth (Plymouth) Plantation in Massachusetts. Settled in 1620, the village was moved several years later more inland after being severely damaged by a hurricane. A journal kept by John Winthrop, the governor of the Massachusetts Bay Colony, along with a book by William Bradford entitled, "Of Plymouth Plantation, 1620-47" and a text written by Rev. Increase Mather in 1684 entitled, "Remarkable Providences", document the widespread devastation in southeastern Massachusetts caused by a great hurricane in 1635. This storm was probably a category 4 (sustained winds of 131 to 155 mph). The next category 4, or possibly 5, to slam into Long Island, New York and New England occurred in 1815. The next storm of such ferocity in that region was the great 1938 hurricane. Rather meticulous documentation on the effects of all of these storms is contained in the excellent book, "The 1938 Hurricane - An Historical and Pictorial Summary" by Dr. William Elliott Minsinger, and is published by the Blue Hill Meteorological Observatory in Milton, Massachusetts.

It was at Milton where the hurricane caused a peak gust of 186 miles per hour. Over 600 people were killed on Long Island and in New England as the storm slashed northward, producing a low barometric pressure reading of 27.94" at Bellport, Long Island. Downtown Providence, Rhode Island was under about 14 feet of water after the storm surge of nearly 30 feet moved in on the Rhode Island shore.

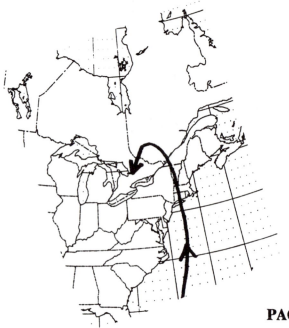

Figure 6. Path of the great 1938 hurricane. Were such a hurricane to strike in the same general area today, with the much greater population than in 1938, the devastation would be catastrophic. Moreover, with the widespread building of homes along the Atlantic shoreline, a storm surge of 20 feet or greater pouring onto the land would inundate a large number of communities.

The steering winds aloft, typically at from about 10.000 through 30,000 feet, have a major impact on the movement of hurricanes as they move northward away form the tropics. When a huge surface and upper-level high pressure system covers much of the North Atlantic Ocean, and extends westward to approximately the shoreline of the east coast, then the clockwise circulation around the high pressure center would tend to help steer the hurricanes around the southern portions of the high towards the east coast, and then up the east coast. Such a pattern caused two hurricanes to strike the northeast within a week of each other in 1955: Connie and Diane.

Conversely, when a trough of low pressure persisted along the east coast in latter August 1995, it appeared to have steered a series of hurricanes away from the east coast. On August 29th, 1995, the weather map showed four tropical storms or hurricanes heading towards the U.S. east coast: Humberto, Iris, Karen and Luis. The southwest-to-northeast steering winds to the east of the trough axis caused Humberto, Iris and then Luis to veer to the north and then northeast, away from the U.S. mainland. Karen was located between Iris and Luis and became absorbed by Iris.

It should be stated here that a tropical storm has a sustained wind of from 39 to 73 mph, a hurricane has a sustained wind of 74 mph or greater. The clear or mostly clear eye of the storm typically develops when the storm's winds reach approximately hurricane force.

But wind and storm surge do not account for all of the hurricane's damage. In June of 1972 a minimal category 1 hurricane named Agnes came up the east coast and then made a left-hand turn in the New York City area, heading westward along the New York-Pennsylvania border. Agnes remained anchored just south of Binghamton, New York and dumped some 15½ inches of rain in about 2 and a half days. This writer was a National Weather Service forecaster stationed at Binghamton during this flash flood. Vivid memories of water rising to the second stories of buildings in Elmira, New York and Wilkes-Barre, Pennsylvania attest to the devastation that a slow-moving hurricane can bring due to its flash flooding rainfall alone. Indeed, that category 1 hurricane, Agnes, is one of the most costly in U.S. history.

Sometimes a hurricane may be accelerating, racing at a pace of 40 to 50 mph or more. Such was the case when Hurricane Hazel in 1954 passed over the Buffalo, New York area -well inland from the ocean- and caused that region's record wind speed of 100 miles per hour.

Eastern Canada is not immune. Particularly strong hurricanes, especially fast-moving ones, have maintained hurricane force winds as they slammed into the maritime provinces. For example, in 1995, parts of coastal Newfoundland received winds over 80 mph from Hurricane Luis.

Although the northeast U.S. and southeast Canada are hurricane-prone, they are not quite as likely to be struck, especially by the severest blows, as much along the east coast as are the middle-Atlantic and southeastern states.   **PAGE 11**

b. middle-Atlantic states hurricanes

Figure 7. The middle-Atlantic states are more prone to direct hits from hurricanes than is the northeast, because of its location in relation to Atlantic-basin hurricanes.

The middle-Atlantic states region receives hurricanes originating over the Atlantic Ocean, and the remains of some Gulf of Mexico hurricanes that eventually move northeast after making landfall in the Gulf states.

The Atlantic-origin storms eventually recurve to the northeast as they move into the middle Atlantic and come under the steering influences of the upper-level winds which during the hurricane season have a predominant westerly component. Thus, many hurricanes move out into the colder north Atlantic waters before striking the northeastern states, but sometimes the recurvature does not occur soon enough to spare the middle-Atlantic states from receiving at least a glancing blow.

The outer banks of North Carolina are particularly hurricane-prone. Hurricane climatology shows us that the area around Cape Hatteras, North Carolina is most likely to be at least affected by passing hurricanes because of its most-eastward protrusion for that region.

In recent years, a quite serious concern has developed for North Carolina and other areas in hurricane-prone regions that have barrier islands off their coasts. Recent land development has led to a significant increase in homes and businesses along the East and Gulf coasts. Many of these people have never experienced a category 4 or 5 hurricane. Many residents have gone through a storm with winds around 100 mph and survived with no more than moderate damage from wind and water. According to two former directors of the National Hurricane Center, Neil Frank and Robert Sheets, this has led to a false sense of security for some people. In other words, if people survive a hurricane of 100 mph, how likely are they to evacuate the area, especially the barrier islands just offshore, if a 160 mph or stronger major hurricane were to move in? For many years, Neil Frank warned residents about the danger.

As a hurricane begins moving in, these barrier islands become separated from the mainland as roads become under water. Then, the only evacuation possible may be "vertical evacuation", in which people move to higher stories in multiple-story structures, and hope that these structures survive.

The middle-Atlantic states have been hit hard by major hurricanes. In 1954, Hurricane Hazel ripped through eastern North Carolina and eastern Virginia, making landfall as a category 4 major hurricane. The region has been hit in the 20th century by several category 3 storms and many lesser hurricanes. In 1955, two category 3s, Connie and Ione, made landfall in North Carolina and caused significant damage throughout the coastal region of the mid-Atlantic states. Diane, a lesser hurricane (category 1), also struck the same region that year. Category 3 hurricanes have sustained winds of from 111 to 130 mph. Thus, three hurricanes struck the mid-Atlantic states within 5 weeks, with Ione being the 4th hurricane to strike there within an eleven month span.

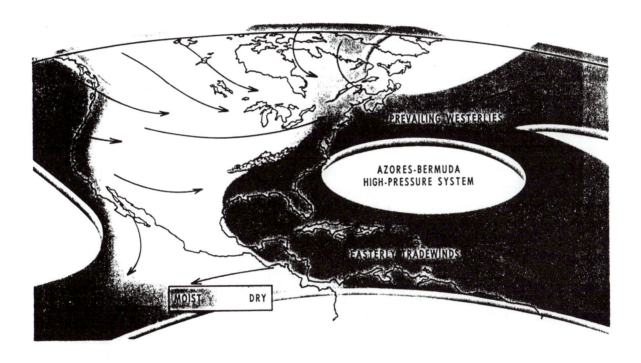

Figure 8. The middle-Atlantic states are most prone to direct hits from Atlantic hurricanes when the Azores-Bermuda high pressure system becomes well-established during the hurricane season. The clockwise flow of air around the high prevents the hurricanes from recurving out to sea while they are still south of the mid-Atlantic region. The steering flow around the south of the center of high pressure has an east-to-west component, thus helping to steer the hurricane towards the mainland.

To illustrate what it is like to withstand tropical storm and hurricane force winds, consider the following.

● An typical adult can usually lean into a 70 mph wind at a 45-degree angle and remain standing.

● It is typically impossible to walk into an 80 mph wind without having support from a hand-rail or some other structure.

● In a sustained 120 mph wind, a flying object such as a tree limb or lawn chair can kill you.

● A 130 mph can lift an average adult off the ground.

● A category 4 hurricane has sustained winds of from 131 to 155 mph, and a category 5 storm has sustained winds in excess of 155 mph. Hurricanes also have gusts even higher. Thus, a category 3 hurricane, with sustained winds of 111 to 130 mph, must be considered as a major hurricane. People who have lived through category 1 (74 to 95 mph) and category 2 (96 to 110 mph) hurricanes but have never gone through a cat. 3 or higher, need to assure that they do not have a sense of false security from having survived a cat. 1 or 2 storm. This is a serious concern among disaster preparedness personnel, as many people do not evacuate threatened areas even with the onslaught of a cat. 3 or higher storm imminent.

Sometimes, a powerful hurricane will take up to some 24 hours before its winds diminish below hurricane strength after moving inland. Such was the case with Hugo in 1989 after it made landfall around Charleston, South Carolina and then moved into the mountains or North Carolina. There was considerable damage in south-central North Carolina from hurricane-force winds.

If not the winds and the storm surge, then the flash flooding may also be life-threatening. In June of 1972, category 1 Hurricane Agnes killed people in the mid-Atlantic states and the northeast, INLAND, from disastrous flooding. In 1969, the remnants of Gulf of Mexico Hurricane Camille caused up to some THIRTY INCHES OF RAIN IN ABOUT SIX HOURS in West Virginia and parts of western Virginia, killing more people there than it did when it came ashore in Mississippi with 200 mph sustained winds.

Nature can also produce the unusual. A hurricane which made landfall around Cape Hatteras, North Carolina in 1839 ran into an unusually early cold high pressure system over the northeast, and produced snow on August 30th in the Catskill Mountains of New York. And in 1971, Hurricane Ginger, which persisted for 27 days, making it one of the longest-lived hurricanes, made some loop-de-loops in her path before eventually hitting North Carolina, Virginia, Delaware, Maryland and Washington, D.C.

And in 1984, Hurricane Diana also made a complete loop off the Carolinas, eventually moving inland on North Carolina, deluging Cape Fear with over 18 inches of rain.

One of the worst hurricanes to affect the region was the Great Hurricane of 1944, which moved from Cape Hatteras to across Chesapeake Bay and continued into New England. This hurricane demolished the Atlantic City, New Jersey boardwalk. The storm took over 400 lives.

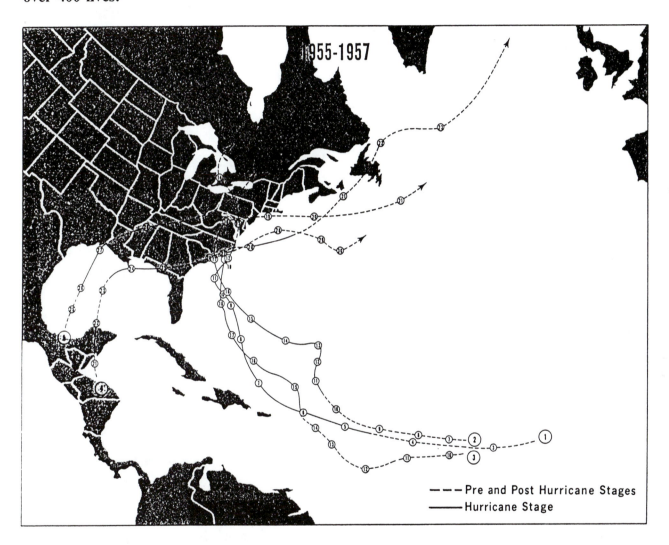

Figure 9. An example of a time period in which the middle-Atlantic states received 3 direct hits from Atlantic hurricanes, and strong winds and heavy rains from Gulf of Mexico hurricanes. (source: National Hurricane Center)

Yet even more prone to hurricanes than the mid-Atlantic states region is the region of the southeastern states, Florida, Georgia and South Carolina.

c. southeastern states hurricanes

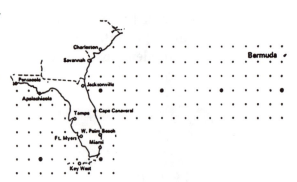

Figure 10. The most vulnerable part of our country to direct onslaught from hurricanes, including major hurricanes, is the southeastern states of the United States, South Carolina, Georgia and Florida, with emphasis on Florida and South Carolina because of their location in relation to the paths of some of the hurricanes. Bermuda is also sometimes struck, often by being in or near the path of some hurricanes whose paths are in the process of recurving to the north and northeast, away from the North American mainland.

Hurricane statistics reveal that the area from Florida to South Carolina can routinely expect to be hit fully or partially by tropical storms and hurricanes, though not every year. Moreover, some of the most powerful hurricanes of all time have struck in this region. The reasons are:

- sea-surface temperatures in the Atlantic in this region are typically in the low to mid 80s F. at least through September, and in sometimes reach the upper 80s on the Gulf of Mexico side of Florida. We know that hurricanes thrive when the sea-surface temperatures are 79°F or higher, with no strong shearing winds aloft from another system, which would work to diminish convection. During the hurricane season, the southeast is usually to the south of many strong shearing systems. Thus, hurricanes tend to maintain or increase their strength and size when passing over these warm waters.

- unless there exists a strong trough over the southeast, the hurricanes' paths will likely not recurve to the northeast as readily as when they are farther north and come more under the influence of the upper-level winds, which most of the time are the "westerlies".

Exacerbating the hurricane problem is the large influx of new residents, especially retirees from more northern regions, to the southeast. Few of these northerners have ever experienced a category 3 or 4 hurricane, and many of these people have bought or built homes along or near the coast. Based on experiences with major hurricanes such as Hugo in 1989 and Andrew in 1992, it is arguable about what percentage of the residents would evacuate their homes if a category 3, 4 or 5 hurricane were to start moving in.

Many homes are constructed to withstand winds of about 100 mph. As winds get above that, roofs start ripping off and windows would likely be smashed. Flying missiles would also contribute to the destruction. Along the coast, the storm surge would come in, sweeping parts of structures and sometimes entire structures apart.

Damage mitigation attempts include installing "hurricane straps" of metal or leather to the house. These are straps that attach to the roof with the other end attaching to the top story of the house. Additional "two-by-sixes" or "two-by-eights" pieces of wood are added to corners of the building, to strengthen structural support. These efforts may help a building that would otherwise receive major damage in a category 2 storm, survive perhaps a category 3 storm.

Here are some examples of major hurricanes that have affected the southeastern states.

● On September 16th, 1700, the storm surge from a major hurricane inundated Charleston, South Carolina with a large loss of life. The same scenario occurred on Sept. 16th-17th, 1713 with an extremely large storm surge. Many vessels were driven ashore during this storm. Charleston was hit by a hurricane in August of 1728, only to be struck again that year on September 14th, with another inundation from the storm surge. In 1752, Charleston was hit by two hurricanes in September, with the one on the 15th damaging or destroying every house constructed of wood. The following year, also on Sept. 15th, Charleston was hit by a hurricane. The weather logs from Charleston, S.C. continue to show significant hurricane strikes through the 18th and 19th centuries, and through the 20th century. A Sept. 10th, 1811 hurricane spawned a tornado which swept through the city. The hurricane of July 1st, 1814 also spawned a tornado, and in the previous year, 1813, a hurricane on August 27th inundated the city again, drowning many people. The late August hurricane of 1893 killed some one thousand people in Georgia and South Carolina, with the storm surge submerging barrier islands. Three major hurricanes struck South Carolina that year. In more recent time, Hurricane Hugo, after severely damaging parts of the U. S. Virgin Islands and northeast Puerto Rico, slammed into South Carolina around midnight, the beginning of Sept. 22nd, 1989 with sustained winds of 135 mph. The eye passed near Charleston. Parts of Charleston County were hit with a storm surge in excess of twenty feet. Shrimp boats were found about one-half mile inland at McClellanville. Another but much smaller hurricane named Iris was to Hugo's southwest, so that the strong anticyclonic (clockwise in the Northern Hemisphere) outflow of air aloft from Hugo sheared Iris and tore her apart, killing her. Iris, too, was heading toward the southeastern states. These hurricane samplings from Charleston, South Carolina demonstrate how vulnerable this area is to direct onslaughts from hurricane, including from major hurricanes.

● On September 18th, 1926, a hurricane's sustained wind at Miami Beach, Florida was 138 mph before the anemometer measuring it blew away.

● A category 4 hurricane struck south Florida in 1928, one of three storms to hit Florida that year, and killed nearly two thousand people.

• In 1935, a CATEGORY 5 HURRICANE swept through the Florida keys, causing widespread destruction. The barometric reading reported in the eye during landfall was 26.35" (892 millibars). Weather records from the 18th through 20th century document many hurricane strikes on Florida, including storms that now would be classified as major hurricanes, i.e., category 3s or greater.

• On the morning of August 24th, 1992, category 4 Hurricane Andrew moved across extreme southern Florida, into the Gulf of Mexico, subsequently moving onshore in diminished yet still powerful intensity in Louisiana. The damage was not from the storm surge, from almost entirely due to the winds. Although sustained winds were of category 4 strength, the peak gusts may have exceeded 175 mph. In terms of 1992 dollars, some 25 billion dollars of damage was caused by Andrew, making it the most costly hurricane in United States history up to that time.

Figure 11. An enhanced infrared satellite image of Hurricane Hugo making landfall on South Carolina. Note the clear eye in the middle of the storm, and the feeder bands of moisture energy to the east of the storm, from the warm ocean source. (source: NOAA)

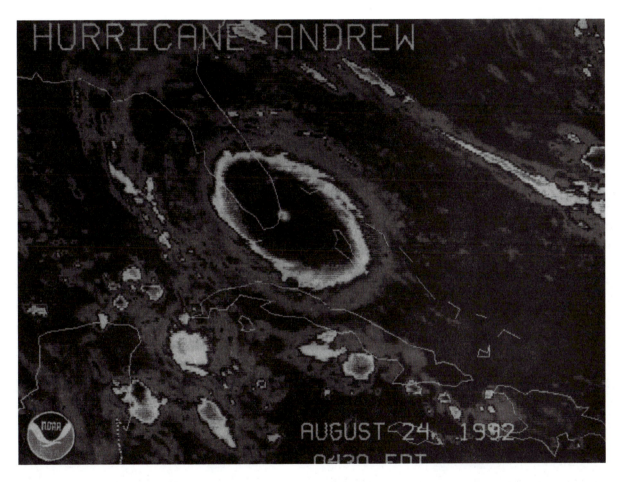

Figure 12. An infrared photo from a weather satellite, showing Hurricane Andrew as he moved ashore on the south Florida coast just south of Coral Gables. Infrared satellite imagery senses the temperature of the tops of clouds. The colder the cloud top temperatures, the higher they are. Different computer-generated shades or colors can be used to highlight the different height bands. Though this was a moderate-sized hurricane, and the strongest winds did not extend outward far from the eye, the storm was the costliest in U.S. history up to that time because it moved into a densely populated area. (source: NOAA)

PAGE 19

d. Gulf of Mexico states hurricanes

Figure 13. Eastern Mexico and the states surrounding the Gulf of Mexico are one of the highest vulnerability zones to being struck by hurricanes. Sometimes that region may not be visited by a tropical cyclone for years, but occasionally multiple hits will occur in one hurricane season, as in the seasons shown below, only two years apart, 1957 and 1959. (source: National Hurricane Center)

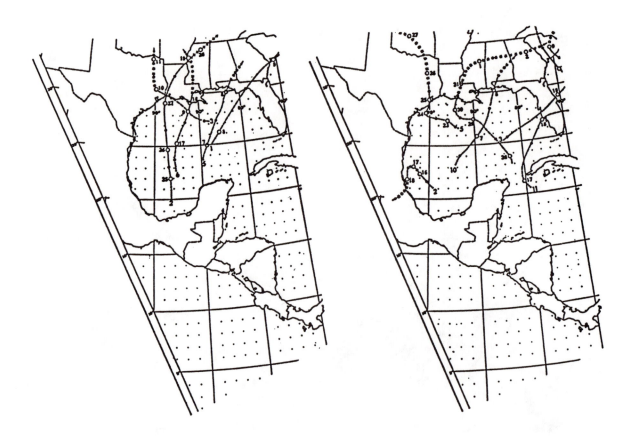

Gulf of Mexico water temperatures are typically in the 80s during the hurricane season. Some sections of the Gulf experience sea-surface temperatures of 86°F (30°C) or higher. If thunderstorms over the Gulf organize into a warm-core circulation, then a tropical depression may form that will grow over these warm waters into a tropical storm or hurricane. Indeed, some of the worst hurricanes in American and Mexican history have been Gulf of Mexico hurricanes, although some of them originated over the Atlantic Ocean and moved into the Gulf.

Here are some notable examples.

THE GREAT GALVESTON, TEXAS HURRICANE DISASTER OF 1900:

(The following description is taken from our book on unusual weather and weather disasters, entitled, "Terror From the Skies!")

The greatest weather disaster in the United States during the 20th century, in terms of lives lost, occurred in 1900 at Galveston, Texas. Excellent eye-witness accounts survive from the head of the Galveston weather bureau office and in an article published in the October 1900 issue of the magazine, "The Western World and American Club Women", published for the 1900 Pan-American Exposition.

Writes Mr. I. M. Cline of the Galveston weather bureau office in 1900, "The hurricane which visited Galveston Island on Saturday, September 8, 1900, is no doubt one of the most important meteorological events in the world's history. The ruin which it wrought beggars description and conservative estimates place the loss of life at the appalling figure, 6,000."

As the worst fury of the storm lashed into Galveston, Mr. Cline continues. "At this time, however, the roofs of houses and timbers were flying through the streets as though they were paper and it appeared suicidal to attempt a journey through the flying timbers. Many people were killed by flying timbers about this time while endeavoring to escape to town."

"The water rose at a steady rate from 3:00 p.m. until about 7:30 p.m., when there was a sudden rise of about four feet in as many seconds. I was standing at my front door which was partly open watching the water which was flowing with great rapidity from east to west. The water at this time was about eight inches deep in my residence and the sudden rise of four feet brought it above my waist before I could change my position." Mr. Cline goes on to state that the water rose to about a 20 foot storm tide, and that debris accumulated as far inland as six blocks from the beach.

He goes on in his account: "The debris was piled up 8 to 15 feet in height. By 8 p.m., a number of houses had drifted up and lodged to the east and southeast of my residence and these with the force of waves acted as a battering ram against which it was impossible for any building to stand for any length of time. And at 8:30 p.m., my residence went down with about 50 persons who had sought it out for safety, and all but 18 were hurled into eternity. Among the lost was my wife who never rose above the water after the wreck of the building. I was drowned beyond consciousness but recovered though being crushed by timbers and found myself clinging to my youngest child who went down with myself and wife."

The wind and waves drifted them into the ocean as they clung to timbers to stay afloat, and the storm later floated them back onto the island.

Several other surviving accounts tell of people up to their necks in water before grabbing onto floating pieces of wood in an attempt to survive the rapidly rising storm surge. Out of a population of 20,000, some 6,000 were killed, mostly drowned by the hurricane's storm surge. Not all bodies were recovered, as many were swept int the Gulf of Mexico.

After reading through several personal accounts of this tragedy while preparing this book, I came across the following about Charlie Gillian, the "widow Ramsey" and her daughter. After relocating Mrs. Ramsey in another building, Charlie Gillian returned to the Ramsey house to get her daughter. The water level at that time was "five feet in the yard". According to the account, the following ensued.

"He and the daughter held hands and started out int the storm, sometimes wading and at other times swimming. Sometimes they would be entirely submerged as a wave rolled over them and at other times they would be lifted off their feet and carried along with the storm. Articles of almost every type were in the water and they were able to dodge most of them. When they had nearly reached 19th Street, they noticed a larger than usual wave approaching them. Charlie saw upon its crest a large piano with its white keys gleaming coming directly toward them. He then told Miss Ramsey to hold tight to him and he dove to allow the wave and piano to pass over them. When he came up Miss Ramsey had lost her hold on him and he could not find her in the darkness. He dived several times but she seemed to have disappeared. When he was about to give up he felt a woman's hand. He brought her to the surface but it was not Miss Ramsey but another girl. He soon found a drifting roof and placed the girl upon it. As he drifted along on the roof he was able to pull four young boys ranging from 4 to 12 years of age from the water and save them. Miss Ramsey's body was never found after the storm."

According to the women's magazine published immediately after the storm, the horror of the hurricane's aftermath was also awesome. The following excerpts are from the magazine.

"Great piles of human bodies, dead animals, rotting vegetation, household furniture and fragments of houses were piled up in confused heaps... The befouling odors were unbearable... Men of strong nerve broke down in their work on surveying the many harrowing sights."

Although natural disasters such as this bring out the best in human nature, they can also bring out the worst in some people. The magazine reported, "There were 100 executions by the vigilante committee in two days." Forty-three people were "found in the ghoulish work of robbing the dead, and twenty-three were killed Sept. 12. From the lamp posts hung their bodies as a warning."

The account gets even more grisly, but for the sake of good taste, enough has been detailed to give you an idea of how a storm surge can devastate a modern community.

Figure 14. An example of a well-organized hurricane to the southeast of Galveston. This storm, Hurricane Anita, headed southwestward into Mexico. The fierce hurricane that hit Galveston, Texas in 1900 had an attack angle such that the storm surge was very high, drowning at least 6,000 people, although updated estimates done in the 1990s conclude that as many as 12,000 people died from the hurricane. (source: NOAA)

On August 18th, 1983, Hurricane Alicia made landfall in the Galveston Island area, producing winds of at least 100 mph even inland at Houston, smashing windows and causing the downtown Houston area to be littered with glass. Hurricane Carla, with sustained winds of 150 mph and gusts to 175 mph, slammed into the same general area on Sept. 11th, 1961, and Hurricane Allen, a huge storm, made landfall near the U.S.-Mexico border on August 9th, 1980, but had weakened considerably from the category 5 status he had for three separate time periods while moving through the Caribbean Sea and then entering the Gulf of Mexico near the northeast tip of Mexico's Yucatan Peninsula, where a barometric reading of 26.55" (899 millibars or hectoPascals) was recorded. By the time Allen made landfall on the North American mainland, the pressure had risen to 27.91" (945 mb).

The coast of Texas, like the coastline from west Florida around the peninsula and up through the North Carolina coast, has been hit routinely by hurricanes.

Figure 15. A visible satellite picture of huge Hurricane Allen off the Yucatan Peninsula at 1731Z (UTC), Aug. 7th, 1980. The storm shows its eye, cyclonic circulation, feeder bands and anticyclonic outflow aloft. (All of these are discussed in later sections of this book.) (source: Robert Case, National Hurricane Center)   **PAGE 24**

Journals, diaries and old news accounts tell of several incidences in which Galveston Island had been completely under water from a hurricane. And back in 1724, the Mission San Antonio de Valero, which is now downtown San Antonio, Texas, was smashed by a "furious hurricane", according to the Franciscan Friars. This caused the friars to move the mission from the banks of the San Antonio River to its current site. It became known as The Alamo. Even though the friars used the word, "hurricane", the storm may have been a tornado or thunderstorm downburst.

Probably the first motion pictures of a hurricane's aftermath were taken by Thomas Alva Edison, who took a train to Texas to film the destruction of Galveston from the 1900 hurricane, with the motion picture camera he invented.

Some of the rainfalls from hurricanes that have moved into Texas have ben impressive. For example, Hurricane Beulah dumped some 30 inches of rain in south Texas in 1967. A 1921 hurricane produced some 35" at Thrall, Texas, and across the Gulf in Florida, a hurricane in 1950 gave Yankeetown about 40 inches of rain within 24 hours! That is close to the average annual rainfall for New York City.

The coasts of all the Gulf of Mexico states have been severely hit by hurricanes. Louisiana, Mississippi and Alabama have experienced some of the greatest hurricanes to storm out from over the Gulf.

On June 27th, 1957, Hurricane Audrey came ashore around Cameron, Louisiana. Although its wind were only 100 mph, a category 2 storm, over 500 people perished. Some of the lives lost were indirectly caused by Audrey. According to research done at Texas A & M University and published in 1975, many residents along the coastline climbed trees to escape the rapidly rising waters of the storm surge. Snakes had also gone up the trees to seek shelter, and they bit many people who subsequently fell out of the trees into the storm surge and drowned. Audrey accelerated northeastward, passing over Rochester, New York and dying in Canada. That hurricane season also saw a hurricane named Carrie come across much of the Atlantic, recurve and cross the Atlantic to strike Great Britain.

THE COMING NEW ORLEANS HURRICANE DISASTER

Perhaps the most vulnerable location along the Gulf of Mexico coast to a disaster from a major hurricane is New Orleans. The reasons are:

●a large population;

●much of the city is below sea-level; and

●category 5 hurricanes have struck the Gulf coast in the past.

Computer simulations have been done to estimate how high the water would be if a category 5 hurricane such as 1969's Camille were to make landfall just west of New Orleans.   The northeast quadrant of the hurricane, in relation to the storm's movement (path), is typically the strongest. If a storm were to move in from the southwest or south, with 200 mph winds and a storm surge in excess of 25 feet, which would be a WORST-CASE SCENARIO, then downtown New Orleans would be under some 25 feet of water.

Storm surges of such great magnitude are uncommon, but when they do happen, the inundation results in devastation. Hurricane Camille had a storm surge of 27 feet, with 15-foot waves on top of it. The Great New England Hurricane of 1938, on Sept. 21st, produced a storm surge that put downtown Providence, Rhode Island under 14 feet of water. A storm surge of 40 feet drowned 300,000 people on Oct. 7th, 1737 at the mouth of the Hooghly River on the Bay of Bengal. A similar storm in 1970 affecting the same general area drowned up to 500,000 people, making it the greatest recorded hurricane disaster in history.

A major reason for the high death tolls is that residents typically have up to about 24 hours advance notice in a hurricane warning. However, a hurricane watch is typically in effect before the warning. The staff at the National Hurricane Center/Tropical Prediction Center in Miami, Florida does an outstanding job of notifying the populace of a threatened area during an approaching hurricane. However, if with 24 hours advance notice in a warning, there is not enough time and not enough roads to evacuate the entire population of New Orleans, even assuming that most of the residents would choose to leave their homes. Logistically, complete evacuation is impossible. Vertical evacuation into upper stories of multiple-story buildings is an option, assuming that the buildings will remain standing and that there are enough of them.

Thus, a category 4 or 5 hurricane will sometime strike the Louisiana coast just west of New Orleans, and a tremendous loss of life and property are inevitable.

Moreover, if the hurricane's storm surge rushes ashore during the time of high tide and especially during the astronomical high tide known as the SPRING TIDE, which occurs when the moon is full or in new moon phase, then the storm surge of water from the ocean (Gulf) is even higher.   PAGE 26

New Orleans was much smaller in the 1700s. Nevertheless, in 1722 a hurricane destroyed the city, which then rebuilt, only to be struck the following year by "a remarkable hurricane (that) nearly destroyed all buildings".

HURRICANE CAMILLE: AN HISTORIC CATEGORY 5 LANDFALL ON THE GULF COAST

One of the most powerful hurricanes in history formed in the Gulf of Mexico off the Yucatan Peninsula in mid-August 1969, intensified rapidly and headed for the Mississippi coast. As the storm neared land, its clear eye shrunk, which was an indication that the swirling winds around the eyewall were intensifying. When the storm made landfall around Pass Christian, its winds were sustained at 200 mph, perhaps 210 mph, with higher gusts. This is probably about as high as hurricane winds can become.

At Pass Christian, residents of the three-story Richelieu Garden Apartment complex were having a "hurricane party" to celebrate the storm. As the storm moved in, the winds increased in fury, sounding more like a tornado. The eye approached, and the dome of water known as the storm surge rose even higher as the high winds and low pressure raised the water level very rapidly when the surge approached the shallow shore water. The storm surge was 27 feet high, and waves 15 feet high were on top of it, battering everything in its path. All the participants in the hurricane party perished except for one woman (although there is one account that says two people may have survived).

The woman floated out the window on top of a mattress, riding the storm surge. This apparently was a third story window. She was rescued after the storm subsided, from the top of a tree.

The apartments were completely washed away. Only a concrete set of first story steps remains, which as of this writing are still there along the Mississippi coast as testimony to the fury of Hurricane Camille.

A colleague of mine, who was in Biloxi during Camille, told me that he saw at least one tornado spawned by the hurricane during the height of the storm. He stated that he was never so scared in his life, which is surely an understatement.

Now consider this: suppose Camille had made landfall only 100 miles to the west. The worst-case scenario would have occurred to submerge New Orleans as water from the Gulf of Mexico would have come surging over the city. Thus, Hurricane Camille on August 17th, 1969, was a frighteningly close call for a holocaust for New Orleans.

Ironically, more people died from the flash floods from Camille much farther inland than did from the wind and storm surge upon her landfall. Camille produced up to thirty inches of rain in about six hours in West Virginia and parts of western Virginia. Every river and stream in the region rapidly flooded. Therefore, even after hurricanes lose most of the fury of their winds after making landfall, they can still be killers through the flash flooding caused by the excessive rainfalls they are capable of producing. Even weak Hurricane Agnes, a minimal category 1 storm in June 1972, was one of the most costly in U.S. history because of its floods brought about by some 2½ days of rainfall, producing up to 15 inches of rain...about half the year's total average...over the Upper Susquehanna River Basin and vicinity of the Southern Tier of New York and eastern and central Pennsylvania.

SUPERHURRICANE GILBERT OF 1988

Figure 16. The visible satellite image of Hurricane Gilbert, taken at 1431Z, Sept. 13th, 1988, as Gilbert was undergoing rapid intensification, with the diameter of his eye shrinking. (source: NOAA)

Sometimes a hurricane may grow so large that, like Allen of 1980, its diameter can span an area equal to the entire Gulf of Mexico. However, for a hurricane to be a powerful category 4 or 5, it need not necessarily be expansive. Typically, however, a powerful hurricane is also large since it has been growing while intensifying.

Hurricane Gilbert came out of the Caribbean, moving into the Gulf of Mexico after slamming Grand Cayman Island and walloping the northeast Yucatan Peninsula.

As Gilbert passed near Grand Cayman Island, near 19.5°N latitude and 83.3°W longitude, it had a barometric pressure of 26.22" or 888 millibars, to set a new Atlantic Basin barometric lowest pressure record, at 2152Z on Sept. 13th, 1988. However, from the Diagnostic Report of the National Hurricane Center for Aug. and Sep. 1988, it is reported: "Although the lowest pressure obtained from reconnaissance aircraft data was 888 mb, an analysis of the data indicates that the 888 mb report occurred during a period when Gilbert's central pressure was falling steadily at a rate of 5 to 6 mb per hour. Therefore, it is likely that the absolute central pressure attained by Gilbert was lower than 888 mb." Thus, the pressure may have bottomed out at just below 26.00".

When Gilbert moved into the northeast Yucatan of Mexico, wind gusts were measured at 218 miles per hour. This landfall weakened the storm somewhat and it later slammed into Mexico still a powerful hurricane.

Computer forecast models projected the storm's movement to turn more northward after it left the Caribbean, but as is the case with some superhurricanes, Gilbert plowed his own path through the environment around him, steadily moving to the west-northwest at essentially the same rate for four days until it hit Mexico south of the Texas border.

The world record, by comparison, for the lowest sea-level atmospheric pressure is 25.69" in the western North Pacific, which is a pressure of 870 mb at sea-level (the pressure you would normally expect almost 5000 feet high).

Thus, the Gulf of Mexico coastline experiences some of the most powerful hurricanes.

e. southwestern states hurricanes

During the hurricane season, more hurricanes form off the west coast of Mexico than in the entire Atlantic Basin including the Caribbean Sea and Gulf of Mexico. A logical question therefore is, "Why doesn't California and other parts of the southwest United States get visited routinely by hurricanes?"

The waters off southwest Mexico and in the Gulf of California are typically above the 79 degree Fahrenheit threshold needed for hurricane genesis. However, over the eastern Pacific during much of the hurricane season, a broad high pressure system usually prevails. In the Northern Hemisphere, the circulation around a high is clockwise. Off the coast of California, this brings low-levels winds that have an easterly component, that is, winds blowing from the northeast, east or southeast. The result is that the surface ocean water along the California coast tends to be moved out, away from the land mass. This water needs to be replaced; therefore, water rises from below. This phenomenon is known as **UPWELLING**. Colder water from below moves up to replace the surface water that has been moved by the prevailing low-level winds farther out to sea. The upwelling brings up nutrients from below which are food which attract certain schools of fish...a boon for anglers and the fishing industry.

Therefore, instead of having warm sea-surface temperatures in the 80s as around Florida, residents of San Diego and Los Angeles Counties, for example, who go into the water for some summer fun, find the water temperatures typically only in the 50s to lower 60s.

Some of the hurricanes that form off the Mexican west coast do head towards coastal California, but as they move over the waters off the northern part of Mexico's west coast, they run into progressively cooler water. The warm ocean needed for convection is replaced by this unfavorable environment, resulting in the rapid dissipation of these hurricanes.

However, very infrequently, hurricanes do survive all the way into the southwestern United States. The following conditions are essential for this to occur:

●the upwelling of cold water must cease temporarily as the air circulation pattern which causes it temporarily relaxes; and/or

●the hurricane must be a fast-mover, heading up along the coast at at least 20 mph; and/or

●the hurricane must be a large and/or intense storm, so that it still has tropical characteristics when reaching the southwest U. S.

Note that the remnants of some eastern Pacific hurricanes move through part of Mexico into Texas, Oklahoma, Kansas and Missouri, for example, still maintaining a circulation, and can produce flash flooding. One of the worst flash floods in Oklahoma's history came from Pacific Hurricane Tico in 1983.

Let us return to the discussion on California and other areas of the southwest. Here are some examples of hurricanes that have hit the southwest.

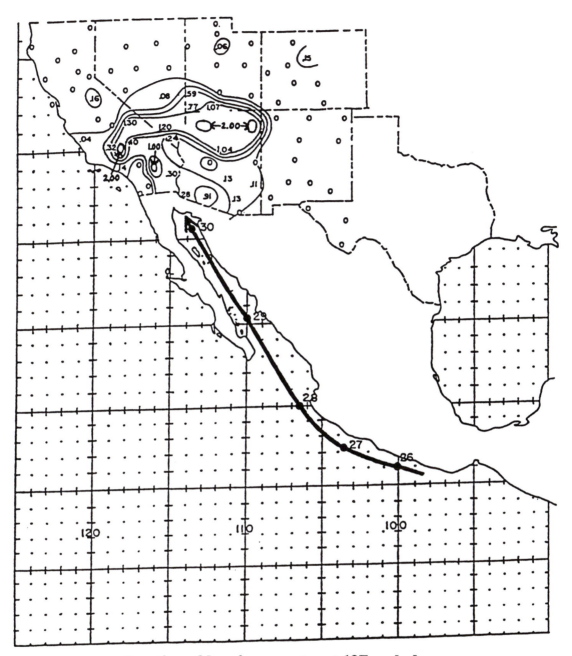

Location of hurricane center at 13Z each day

Figure 17. The path of a hurricane that moved over the warm waters of the Gulf of California, moving into the southwest United States. The map also shows rainfall amounts from this hurricane of September 26-30, 1932.

The above situation is rare. The storm would need to be a well-organized hurricane with its eye moving directly up the middle of the Gulf of California. This happened in 1932.

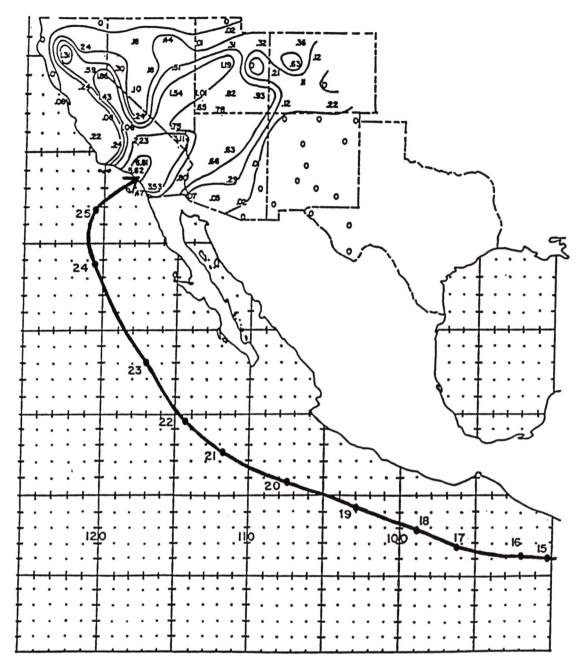

Location of hurricane center at 12Z each day

Figure 18. A hurricane that moved ashore on the southern California coast. The hurricane of September 15-25, 1939 moved inland between San Diego and Los Angeles. The maximum sustained winds from a tropical storm striking the southwest were 46 to 52 mph south of Los Angeles from this storm on Sept. 25th, 1939, and in the Imperial Valley of California and the Lower Colorado River Valley on Sept. 10th, 1976. The highest wind gust from a hurricane in the southwest was of hurricane intensity, 76 mph, at Yuma. Arizona on the morning of Sept. 10th, 1976.

PAGE 32

f. Hawaiian hurricanes

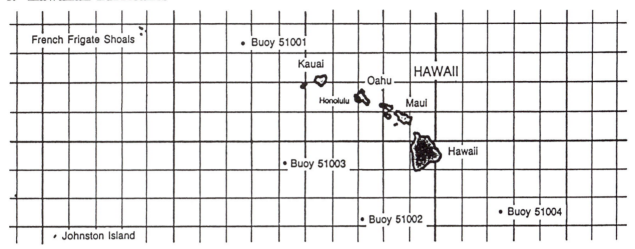

Figure 19. Any of the islands of the Hawaiian Islands chain is vulnerable to a catastrophic blow from a category 5 superhurricane.

The Hawaiian Islands came close to being struck by two category 5 hurricanes within about as many weeks in the 1994 hurricane season. Occasionally, a hurricane with its origins off the Mexican west coast will stay sufficiently south and over very warm water as it works its way westward across the Pacific, intensifying to category 3 or 4 intensity. Three such powerful hurricanes moved south of the Hawaiian Island chain in 1994, two of them being category 5 superhurricanes.

One of these storms, Hurricane John, in August and September, lasted for 31 days. When John was passing some 300 miles south of Hilo, Hawaii, he had sustained winds of 170 miles per hour with gusts to 200 miles per hour. A storm of such intensity would have devastated the part or parts of Hawaii it could have moved through.

Some of these storms, as they cross the International Dateline at 180°W longitude, then enter the western Pacific Ocean and are given new names, along with the nomenclature of the western Pacific for tropical cyclones, i.e., they are then called typhoons.

Fortunately, the Hawaiian Islands are relatively small, and usually to the north of the paths of most hurricanes coming from the east. Moreover, most of the Mexican hurricanes die before even getting close to Hawaii, with many of them heading northwestward onto colder, sometimes upwelling, water. However, hurricanes also form in the central Pacific, and these pose a greater risk for Hawaii.

Overall, the frequency of being hit is relatively low. The frequency of having a category 4 or 5 hurricane is also low. Therefore, the likelihood that Hawaii would be hit by a cat. 4 or 5 storm is small indeed. The first close call in decades was in 1994. Thus, the potential exists, albeit low.

Hurricanes that have struck Hawaii in recent decades include:

HURRICANE HIKI, which affected Kauai from August 15th through 17th, 1950. The highest observed sustained winds on land were 68 mph.

HURRICANE DELLA, on September 4th, 1957, did not directly affect Hawaii, but did strike the French Frigate Shoals, between Hawaii and Midway Island, with winds of 82 mph and gusts to 109 mph.

HURRICANE NINA, on December 1st and 2nd, 1957, some three months after Della, passed 100 miles southwest of Kauai, but the island reported gusts to 92 mph.

HURRICANE DOT, on August 6th, 1959, also struck Kauai. Dot had 81 mph winds with gusts reported to 103 mph.

HURRICANE FICO, affected the big island of Hawaii from July 18th through 20th, 1978, but winds reached only around 60 mph in gusts.

HURRICANE IWA was a powerful storm that passed to the south of Oahu and to the west of Kauai on November 23rd and 24th, 1982. Honolulu was buffeted by high winds and drenching rains, and mountainous regions had mudslides from the flash flooding. The highest reported winds on land were 65 mph with gusts to 117 mph. Fortunately, the loss of life was low..one death...but property damage was about one quarter billion dollars.

HURRICANE ESTELLE, on July 22nd, 1986, affected Maui and Hawaii. Highest sustained winds were 55 mph. Estelle brushed the coastline of Hawaii, generating twenty-foot high waves.

HURRICANE INIKI was one of the most powerful tropical cyclones to hit part of the Hawaiian Islands. The storm was moving west-northwest, south of the Islands, and appeared to be heading towards the western Pacific where it would then be classified as a typhoon. However, as it moved to the south of Kauai, the storm made a sharp right turn, heading northward, and smashed directly into Kauai on September 11th, 1992. Besides devastating the tourism business temporarily, Iniki demolished the set of "Jurassic Park", the science fiction thriller movie being filmed on Kauai by Steven Spielberg. Ironically, this was the last set of scenes that need to be filmed for the motion picture when Iniki struck destroying the set.

Hurricane Iniki affected Oahu and Kauai, but Kauai was especially hard hit. Reported sustained winds hit 92 mph and gusts reached 143 mph, but where the storm made landfall, she had sustained winds of 140 mph with gusts to 175 mph, classifying it as a category 4 hurricane. 35-foot high waves crashed onto the shore. Eight people lost their lives and damage was about two billion dollars.

Figure 20. Hurricane Iwa on November 23rd, 1982. Her eye was to the west of Kauai at this time. Iwa's eye had come to within 25 miles of the northwest coast of Kauai. (source: NOAA)

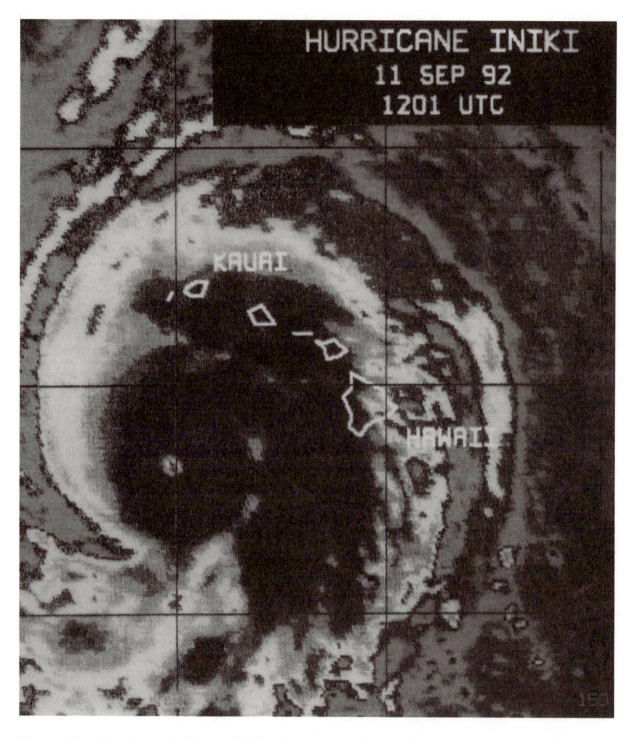

Figure 21. Hurricane Iniki at 1201Z, September 11th, 1992, as she makes a right hand turn and heads straight for Kauai. This hurricane is a huge, well-organized, category 4 storm. (source: NOAA)

g. northwest states and Alaska hurricanes

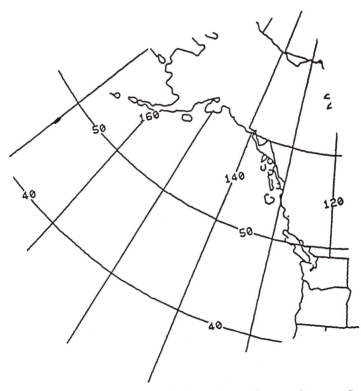

Figure 22. For as long as weather records have been kept, the northwest states and Alaska have never been struck by a hurricane coming up from the Mexican west coast. However, typhoons from the western Pacific Ocean have on rare occasion affected these regions.

Consider the Atlantic Basin. Occasionally, a large and powerful hurricane will last after recurvature of its path, crossing the Atlantic Ocean, and if no farther north than Scandinavia, will move into western Europe. The storm may have both tropical and nontropical (called "extratropical") characteristics (discussed later in section 3e). In the Pacific Basin, large and powerful typhoons, often moving past Japan, will move northeastward over the warm Kuroshio Current. The Kuroshio Current in the Pacific is quite similar to the Gulf Stream in the Atlantic. Both are warm currents of water which originate in the western part of their respective equatorial current, and transport warm water to higher latitudes. When a hurricane takes a route over this current for quite a distance, it is less likely to weaken, and may even strengthen, especially in lower latitudes, because the warm sea temperatures act to supply energy to the hurricane as warm, moist air feeds into the storm.

The Gulf Stream heads towards Iceland, and the Kuroshio Current heads towards the Aleutian Islands of Alaska.

Has a typhoon actually ever made it entirely across the Pacific Ocean to strike the western United States or western Canada? Obviously, if it does happen, the event would be a rather rare occurrence.

One such rare event has been documented by the newspaper, the Oregonian. In early October 1962, Typhoon Frieda formed in the South China Sea, touched land briefly, and then headed for her journey across the Pacific. Frieda was expected to die as she moved northeastward towards colder waters. However, she was maintaining a path directly over the warm Kuroshio Current, which may have been unusually warm that year.

As Frieda began to head into progressively cooler waters, she took a surprise turn to the south. On October 10th, 1962, she was centered 300 miles south of Adak, a far western Aleutian Island. Its central pressure had risen to 29.35", but she was still a typhoon (hurricane) and was taking an unusual path to the southeast, towards the U.S. northwest coast. The storm apparently moved to where a jet-stream aloft accelerated the typhoon towards the North American coastline.

Late on October 11th, as Frieda approached California from some 700 miles west of San Francisco, she turned northeastward, heading for the Oregon coast. Her barometric pressure had actually dropped some, to 29.21".

The weather office at Portland, Oregon, then known as the United States Weather Bureau (the name change to National Weather Service occurred in 1970), issued the following statement at 10:10 a.m. local time on October 12th, 1962:

"A very deep, vigorous storm that is the remnant of a Pacific Ocean tropical storm is moving in a northeasterly direction and is expected to be centered over the ocean near the mouth of the Columbia River this afternoon."

The advisory went on to inform the public that warnings for winds just below hurricane intensity were in effect for the coast from northern California through Washington, and that very heavy rainfall was expected.

Since the storm at this time was still a typhoon but with some extratropical characteristics, a hurricane warning for the northwest coast would also have been appropriate, but would also have been unprecedented. There has never been a hurricane warning due to a typhoon that originated thousands of miles away across the largest ocean on earth!

As the hurricane moved in, its tropical characteristics became evident. Bands of squalls moved onshore, each band stronger than the previous, until the steadily increasing sustained damaging winds arrived as the storm's center approached the Oregon coast. The temperature rose markedly as the tropical air of the typhoon moved into the area.

PAGE 38

The fierce storm was unlike any of the other Pacific storms that had struck Oregon before. The characteristics were that of a hurricane moving in, with the storm coming from the southwest, acting like a Gulf of Mexico hurricane heading northeastward towards the Louisiana coast.

Looking back at weather maps following the storm, Typhoon Frieda made landfall in southern Oregon, with a pressure of 28.84". The weather bureau office at Portland reported a peak gust of 104 miles per hour. In the Portland area itself, the wind reached 116 mph.

In local Oregonian weather lore, the storm became known as the Columbus Day Storm. Eugene, Oregon had 86 mph winds, and Salem had 70 mph.

Two meteorologists for the Portland weather office stated at the time, as they researched this storm, that it was hard to say what the Typhoon Frieda effect was on this storm. They stated, "We believe this could be a factor, possibly an important one, but it would be difficult to prove due to the lack of upper air observations around the storm."

The storm killed 23 people and caused widespread damage in western Oregon. Coastal Washington also received hurricane force winds, but Frieda was weakening as she moved inland. Frieda moved into British Columbia.

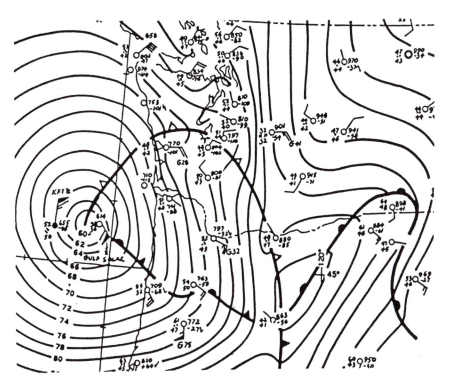

Figure 23. The surface weather map at 4 p.m. Pacific Standard Time, Oct. 12th, 1962. With fronts analyzed with the storm, Typhoon Frieda by this time had both tropical and extratropical characteristics.

For as long as weather records have been kept, Alaska had never been hit by a hurricane or typhoon that maintained pure tropical characteristics. Even when Pacific typhoons remain strong storms as they accelerate northeastward through the west and central Pacific, they have cold air entraining into them as they move into and through progressively colder environments. These systems are in the process of transforming from warm-core tropical storms with a warm high pressure system above them, into an extratropical low pressure system with a low or trough above them in the upper troposphere. At best, the storms would be hybrid when reaching southern or western Alaska or western Canada.

In 1995, a powerful typhoon named Oscar brushed Japan and passed by the south coast of Alaska. Meteorological research requires detailed surface and upper-air observations of such systems to determine how much if any tropical characteristics remain. There is no priority (and no money!) to fly hurricane hunter planes into remnants of hurricanes and typhoons even when they still maintain sustained hurricane force winds but are no longer classified as tropical cyclones.

There also occurs a unique storm called an Arctic Hurricane which affects the Arctic during its winter, and has surprisingly convective origins. It has also been referred to as a type of "polar low". This storm is discussed in section 3f.

3. HURRICANES ELSEWHERE

a. Caribbean, Central American and extreme South American hurricanes

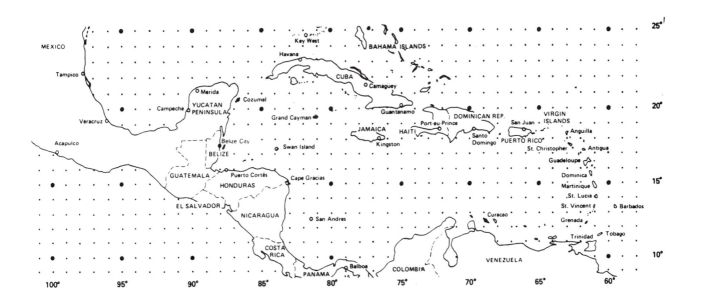

Figure 24. The region from the Caribbean through Central America is highly vulnerable to hurricanes. On the Atlantic side, some of the most powerful hurricanes of all time have moved through this region.

In the Northern Hemisphere tropics, the predominating direction for the low-level winds is from the northeast, and are called the Trade Winds, from the old trading days from the 1500s through 1800s, since all goods were brought in and out by ships utilizing these winds. In the Southern Hemisphere tropics, the prevailing direction for these winds is from the southeast. These winds are part of the general circulation of the atmosphere.

Therefore, with northeast winds in the tropics north of the equator, and southeast winds in the tropics south of the equator, the air is converging in the vicinity of the equator. During the Northern Hemisphere hurricane season, large areas of high pressure predominate in middle latitudes in the Atlantic and in the Pacific. The clockwise flow around them also means that low-level winds will have a predominating easterly component to them as we approach the Northern Hemisphere tropics.

Because air is not destroyed or created in this convergence process, it has to go somewhere while converging. When air converges near the surface it is forced upward. The zone of convergence and rising air is called the:

INTERTROPICAL CONVERGENCE ZONE, or ITCZ.

For reasons not yet fully understood, the ITCZ's main axis of convergence and lift is displaced by up to ten or somewhat more degrees latitude to the north during the Northern Hemisphere hurricane season. This region of rising air leads to frequent thunderstorm development. Often, the thunderstorms will organize into large masses known as **mesoscale convective systems (MCSes)**, forming over the warm water. The warmer and the more moist the air is, with the greatest lift, then, if the air is unstable (cools off at a sufficient rate as we rise through the troposphere), the thunderstorms will form. Many of these MCSes form over equatorial Africa, and move off that continent's west coast into the Atlantic ITCZ as seedlings for potential tropical storms. Indeed, many of the superhurricanes had their origins this way, so that they can spend about a week moving across the tropical Atlantic while intensifying. When they hit land, they deintensify. (Details of the hurricane's life cycle are documented in chapters 4 and 5.)

Thus, locations such as the Windward and Leeward Islands in the Caribbean, and all other locations in the Caribbean have been hit often by hurricanes, including by superhurricanes (categories 4 and 5).

Mexico is vulnerable on both coasts, since hurricanes can enter the country from the Caribbean, the Gulf of Mexico, the Pacific Ocean and the Gulf of California. More hurricanes form off the west coast of Mexico than in the entire Atlantic Basin, which includes the Caribbean Sea and Gulf of Mexico; however, most of these head out into the Pacific, spending their lives at sea.

The first documented hurricane in the New World was by Christopher Columbus and his crew when they ran into a rare out-of-season hurricane in one of their journeys in the 1490s. Moreover, Santo Domingo in the Caribbean reported being struck by hurricanes in June and August of 1494 and in October of 1495. In 1498, a Spanish fleet was damaged when it ran into a hurricane while en route from Cuba to Spain.

In 1530, three hurricanes within 6 weeks devastated San Juan, Puerto Rico, to be followed seven years later by three hurricanes within two months.

In August of 1591, an entire fleet perished in a hurricane while en route from Havana, Cuba to Spain, drowning some 500 people. There are many ships buried in and near the Caribbean from the 16th through 19th centuries, including many with gold, silver and gold coins such as Spanish pieces-of-eight.

A hurricane on October 7th, 1670 drove a British fleet ashore at Jamaica.

And a late season hurricane in November of 1744 struck Cuba and caused, according to the surviving documentation, a tremendous explosion and infestation of the worm population. The event was termed a plague of worms.

Accounts of numerous ships lost in the Leeward and Windward Islands through the centuries attest to the frequency and intensity of these storms.

On June 21st, 1791, some three thousand people perished in a hurricane that lashed Cuba; many of these deaths may have come from the storm surge.

The record shows that Puerto Rico has been hit often, and that a good number of the storms were very intense. A quasi-stationary hurricane blasted the island for some 50 hours in August of 1807. In fact, in the period from 1804 through 1819, Puerto Rico was struck many times by hurricanes: in 1804, 1806, 1807, 1809, twice in 1812, in 1813, 1814, 1816, 1818 and 1819. The 1816 hurricane may have been a category 5, since it virtually destroyed everything. The 1819 storm was also quite severe.

Suppose that Puerto Rico were to endure another such period of high frequency of hurricane strikes, with the much greater population on the island now? It happened before; a similar scenario can not be considered improbable.

In an August 1835 hurricane in Antigua, the barometer fell one inch in 87 minutes.

Thus, by chronicling some of the earliest recorded storms in the Caribbean, it is obvious that the region is vulnerable to being ravaged by hurricanes, including by category 5 storms.

In more recent decades, Hurricane Janet of 1955, a superhurricane with 200 mile-per--hour winds, plowed into Mexico and Belize. On September 26th, the crew of a hurricane hunter reconnaissance aircraft was killed as the airplane crashed into the ocean in the hurricane. Hurricane hunter planes enter the calm eye from the eyewall which contains the most intense winds, at an angle, rather than, in Janet's case, flying directly from 200 mph sustained winds to a sudden calm, and then back again from the calm eye into suddenly 200 mph sustained howling fury.

A somewhat amusing story came out of Swan Island, which was devastated as Janet passed to its south. Swan Island is south of Cuba, and in 1955 had a United States weather office and a federal aviation unit located there. This story was told to me in 1973 or '74 by a meteorological technician who was stationed on Swan Island when Janet struck.

The duty there was considered "isolated duty", which meant "single people only". Since it was illegal to have alcohol ("booze") on the federal installation, the spirits had to be smuggled in from Puerto Rico when the occasional supply ship or plane would arrive.

PAGE 43

The personnel would hide the contraband, mostly rum, burying it in the sand, and would create treasure maps showing its locations. On weekends, some of it would be dug up and enjoyed by the weather and the aviation staffs. When Hurricane Janet hit, it destroyed every structure on Swan Island except for the aviation building, which is where everyone took shelter and survived. The big tragedy, according to the meteorological technician, is that Janet's storm surge washed up thousands of dollars of rum from the sand and took it all out to sea.

In September of 1988, category 5 Hurricane Gilbert plowed through the Caribbean and eventually made landfall on Mexico's Yucatan Peninsula (see figure 16 for a visible satellite image of Gilbert at his peak intensity). Winds gusted to 218 mph at landfall.

The year 1995 had an interesting hurricane season. There was an unusually large number of storms early in the season - 12 tropical storms or hurricanes by August 28th - and at one time four tropical storms or hurricanes were on the weather map simultaneously. Tropical Storm Karen was between Hurricane Iris to her northeast and Hurricane Luis to her southwest. Karen was absorbed by the circulation Iris.

In 1995, a large trough of low pressure along the east coast steered this conveyor belt of hurricanes out to sea. Had this not happened, the United States east coast would have endured multiple strikes from hurricanes in rapid succession, with some of these storms being quite strong, and some being rather large. The Caribbean was hit hard.

I was able to receive messages over the internet from survivors of Hurricanes Luis and Marilyn as they moved through the Caribbean. Backup power supplies and some of the phone communications staying up allowed for "as-it-is-happening" reporting.

Here are some excerpts from Antigua as Hurricane Luis passed over in early September 1995.

"It is Tues., 5th Sept., at 10:45 a.m. I'm writing from Cable and Wireless, Antigua. Antigua is right in the path of Luis and is looking like it's going to be hit VERY HARD. Winds are in the 120+ mph range, gusting over 140 mph."

"As I look out over the Cable and Wireless Compound, I can see parts of people's roofs in the car park. The wind is whistling by and the rain is "falling" horizontally..."

"All government utilities have been disconnected in preparation for Luis, and so there is no power or water..."

"The worst thing about this hurricane is that the second half (after the eye has passed) looks to be much larger than the first half. Not only that, but the storm has slowed down from 12 mph to 9 mph, meaning that it will have even more time to cause havoc..."

Many tourist resorts on Antigua were flattened. Parked airplanes were blown off the airport taxiways and runways.

Farther south, on the Caribbean island of Montserrat, the population was in double misery. The Soufriere Hills Volcano was erupting about every 8 hours, and people had been evacuated away from the southern part of the island near the volcano, including from the largest city, Plymouth, to the north end of the island. Then the hurricane passed to the north. Residents were fearful of returning to their homes in the south for shelter because of the hurricane. On the internet came reports such as this one:

"Trees are coming down and the electricity poles are swaying." Then roofs started coming off. Fortunately, Luis did not strike Montserrat with his full fury, but Antigua to the north suffered a direct hit.

However, several days later, on September 14th and 15th, Hurricane Marilyn made a direct hit on Montserrat and proceeded to devastate the U.S. Virgin Islands.

Internet reports from Montserrat during Marilyn included these comments:

"Eating by flashlight, some rain coming through the roof. Need to move computers downstairs. Some thunder and lightning just became noticeable."

"..technical college has lost some roof which is blocking the road...I am surprised at the damage..."

Volcano evacuees, after fighting with Hurricane Luis, returned to their homes in the south of Montserrat for shelter from Hurricane Marilyn, despite the danger of an imminent volcanic eruption. Fortunately, the volcano remained relatively calm during Marilyn.

Luis also killed Marilyn. As Luis, which was a large hurricane, moved north-northeastward off the U.S. east coast, it churned up a large expanse of sea-surface, allowing colder water from below to rise to the surface to replace the warm surface water that was pushed away. Marilyn followed closely Luis' path off the east coast, passing over this pool of colder water and weakened. Oceanographic observations show that water temperatures in the low to mid 80s were temporarily replaced with a pool of water temperatures in the mid to upper 70s. Recall that hurricanes typically need ocean surface temperatures of 79 degrees F. or higher to sustain themselves or grow, when no other weather system is acting to shear apart the top of the storm through strong winds aloft acting oppositely to the hurricane's winds.

Marilyn could have actually regenerated had she moved into a more favorable environment over warmer water. As she was dissipating, Marilyn was forced southeastward by a strong high pressure system to her north and a trough to her northeast. She was expected to move southward and eventually southwestward, which would have placed her over water with temperatures in the middle 80s, but she died before reaching the agreeable waters.

In conclusion, the region from the Caribbean Sea westward through Mexico and the rest of Central America are quite vulnerable to hurricanes, including major hurricanes, as is proven by documentation from the days of Columbus through today.

b. western Pacific and eastern Asian typhoons

In the western Pacific, hurricanes are called typhoons. (The word history of the word "typhoon" is documented on page 5.) Since the term "hurricane" was derived from a Carib Indian word, it is used in the Atlantic Basin and eastern and central Pacific only.

Typhoons can be larger and sometimes more powerful than their Atlantic siblings, because, depending on where in the Pacific Ocean they form, typhoons may have a larger reach of ocean over which to travel and intensify when they are in the tropics over warm surface water.

Typhoons form in the western Pacific Basin in the Northern Hemisphere, and some of them originate in the central tropical Pacific. There are also cases of hurricanes forming off the Mexican Pacific coast, heading westward across the International Dateline, and then being reclassified as typhoons with new names from the typhoon list of names.

It is somewhat aggravating that, for climatological categorizing, the hurricane/typhoon does not keep its name of origin when it crosses into another political territory. Hurricanes have crossed Central America from the Atlantic to the Pacific, and are immediately assigned a name from the eastern Pacific list for that year. This obfuscates tagging the storm throughout its history from origin to dissipation.

Consider an extreme theoretical example. An "easterly wave" (to be discussed later) or a mesoscale convective system (MCS) forms over southern India (or it may be the MCS remnants of an Indian Ocean tropical cyclone), works its way westward into equatorial Africa, subsequently moving off the African west coast and becoming a tropical depression. As the seedling moves westward over warm, tropical waters, it becomes a tropical storm and then hurricane. The storm crosses the tropical Atlantic Ocean into the southern Caribbean Sea as it becomes a category 4, then 5, hurricane. Let's call our storm, Barbara.

Hurricane Barbara smashes into Nicaragua with 200 mph winds, and crosses the country, reemerging over warm tropical waters off Nicaragua's west coast after diminishing to a 120 mph hurricane due to its passage over the mountainous terrain. Barbara is still a hurricane, but is now known as Hurricane Jose.

Jose strengthens as she/he moves westward to a point a few hundred miles south of the eastern Hawaiian Islands.

As Jose moves past the Dateline, it becomes Typhoon Mary. Mary eventually passes directly over Tokyo with 200 mph winds as she devastates Japan. Next, Mary accelerates rapidly northeastward to be south of the Aleutian Islands, rapidly becoming a hybrid tropical and extratropical storm, while still packing 100 mph winds.

As Barbara-Jose-Mary lashes into northern California, it is a powerful extratropical low pressure system, bringing excessive rainfall and 100 mph winds. The storm works its way into the Central Plains, after expending much of her tropical moisture in the western United States, and her sustained winds have diminished to about 50 mph with gusts around hurricane strength. Now, high dewpoint air from the Gulf of Mexico is being drawn into the eastern side of the storm, rising over the colder air to its north. The storm is reintensifying.

As the low passes through southern New England, an early Autumn mass of cold air acts with the low to produce a late September snowstorm of over 120 inches (ten feet), with the gale wind creating exceptionally high drifts which bury two-story homes.

The huge and blocking high pressure system to the storm's north forces it to move southeastward. Eventually, the storm is near the U.S. Virgin Islands and has become quasi-stationary. It begins to reacquire tropical characteristics as it sits over the 84 to 87 degree sea-surface.

Soon, the storm spins up to a tropical storm, and 24 hours later is a hurricane. Now, the storm is Hurricane Jeannie.

Jeannie becomes a category 3 storm with sustained winds of 130 mph and eventually turns to the west, then northwest, paralleling the east coast of Florida. Jeannie moves over Cape Hatteras with 130 mph winds and gusts to 175 mph, and then passes up Chesapeake Bay, over New Jersey and New York City and across southern New England. Winds remain just above 100 mph since strong feeder bands from over the ocean maintain much of the storm's energy source.

Jeannie is shunted by a persistent high pressure system to her north, and moves east-southeastward across the Atlantic. Before reaching the Cape Verde Islands, Jeannie turns northeastward, still a hurricane, and strikes Great Britain with 100 mph winds.

Eventually, Jeannie is again an extratropical low as it moves across Poland and eventually across Siberia, emerging into the Pacific near St. Paul Island, Alaska as a powerful snow, rain and wind storm, and eventually works its way to the Canadian coast and then becomes what is known as an "Alberta Clipper", bringing blizzard conditions to parts of Montana, Wyoming and the Dakotas.

And so the saga continues. The storm is Barbara-Jose-Mary-extratropical-Jeanne-extratropical, but at least during the storm's lifespan from Hurricane Barbara through Typhoon Mary, should not she have always been permitted to retain her name, Barbara? Tokyo would have been struck by Hurricane Barbara with her origins over India, rather than by Typhoon Mary.

In the Atlantic Basin, a large number of hurricanes is likely in a season when the weather is very wet over equatorial Africa, since many more MCSes than average will form over this part of Africa, and many of these will survive to make it off the west coast of that continent. This happened, for example, in the 1995 hurricane season. In the western Pacific, however, most of the typhoon seedlings originate over the warm tropical water. There as over the Atlantic, the water temperature typically needs to be at or above the threshold value of 79 degrees Fahrenheit for tropical cyclone genesis. Moreover, the environment favorable for typhoon development must not have another weather system that yields winds aloft that would shear the tops of any developing tropical wave or depression.

Some of the most powerful tropical cyclones on earth occur in the typhoon part of the Pacific. The Philippines, Vietnam, south and east China and Japan, as well as islands in the tropical western North Pacific, are often affected by these typhoons.

Because of the large expanse of warm water in the Pacific, much more in area than in the Atlantic, the typhoons have the potential to grow into large and intense storms, because they may not strike land as soon their Atlantic Basin siblings may.

Thus, although the Saffir-Simpson hurricane intensity scale was developed for the Atlantic Basin hurricanes, if it is used for the Pacific typhoons, we find that there are likely more stronger category typhoons than there are Atlantic Basin hurricanes.

Indeed, as of this writing, Typhoon Tip, in October 1979, holds the record for the lowest sea-level atmospheric pressure recorded on earth: 25.69", which is 870 millibars (hectoPascals). This was recorded over the western North Pacific at 16.7°N, 137.8°E. When a typhoon spins up to such extreme intensity, its eye shrinks as air rotates violently around it. The eye of such typhoons may be no more than 10 miles (some 16 kilometers) across.

Some typhoons have had diameters in excess of 500 miles (800 km), which, if centered in the Gulf of Mexico, would cover the entire Gulf and would affect the coastline all around it. Hurricane Allen in 1980 was about that size. Allen also had an extremely low pressure, 26.55" (899 mb), when he was moving through the Caribbean Sea (this was reported at 21.6°N, 86.2°W).

Thus, the east coast of North America and the east coast of Asia are vulnerable to tropical cyclones originating either in the tropics or in conditions that are tropical.

c. Australian region cyclones

Surprisingly, since the Southern Hemisphere has more ocean than has the Northern Hemisphere, hurricanes are not as numerous there, but they do occur in select places.

Since the Coriolis force in the Southern Hemisphere deflects the wind to the left, the circulation around low pressure systems including tropical storms is clockwise. In the vicinity of Australia, these storms are called CYCLONES or TROPICAL CYCLONES. The term "willy-willy", which may at some time in the past have been used by some people in Australia for a hurricane, is a term used to describe a whirlwind, and if used at all nowadays, it refers to very small whirlwinds such as dust-devils, and is not used for a hurricane.

Occasionally, a tropical cyclone strikes Australia, coming in from the tropics to the north. Darwin, for example, on the north coast facing the Indian Ocean, was ravaged by a tropical cyclone in the 1980s. Australia's north coast is the most vulnerable part of the continent.

In 1881, an intense hurricane struck Cossack, Australia in January, in the Southern Hemisphere summer, with a central pressure of 27.00" (914 millibars). In January of 1959, a tropical cyclone named Beatrice struck New Caledonia, with a barometric pressure of 27.73 " (939 mb) reported at Poindimie.

d. Indian Ocean cyclones

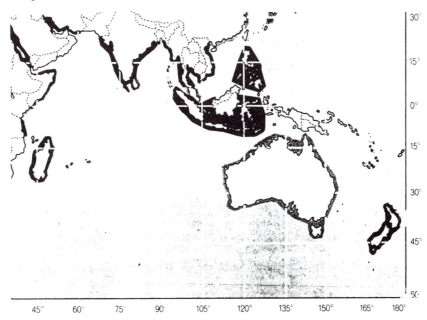

Figure 25. The Indian Ocean between Africa and Australia generates hurricanes in both hemispheres.

Australia is not the only area vulnerable to Indian Ocean hurricanes. Occasionally, they affect east Africa.

In March 1968, a tropical cyclone named Monica hit Rodriguez Island in the southwest Indian Ocean with a pressure of 27.58" (934 mb).

Back in the Northern Hemisphere, a tropical cyclone in May of 1963 to the southeast of the Arabian Peninsula produced a pressure of 27.97" (947 mb) at 14.8°N, 60.1°W.

A tropical cyclone moved inland at False Point, India in September 1885 with a pressure of 27.14" (919 mb), and one struck Chittagong, Bangladesh in May of 1963, with a ship somewhat south of there reporting a 27.17" (920 mb) pressure.

The greatest weather disasters of all time occurred in the Bangladesh coastal region. On October 7th, 1737, an intense hurricane hit at the mouth of the Hooghly River on the Bay of Bengal, producing a storm surge of forty feet which drowned some 300,000 people. And in November of 1970, a similar storm in the same general area also produced a major storm surge which killed 200.000 to 300,000 people in Bangladesh, conservatively estimated, and may have drowned as many as 500,000.

A large population lives on islands that are just above sea-level. The fertile land is excellent for farming and ranching. Even if warnings had a 24 hour lead time in 1970, it is physically impossible to evacuate millions of people from the coast and coastal islands. There are insufficient roads, airports and docks. Moreover, people do not want to abandon their farms and other property. As a consequence, up to one-half million people perished in modern times from one intense hurricane.

Recall that in the United States in September 1900, from 6 thousand to 12 thousand people were swept into the Gulf of Mexico at Galveston, Texas from a hurricane's storm surge, which is the greatest weather disaster for the United States as of this writing.

Our tragedy was 6,000 to 12,000 lives lost in one hurricane, in 1900, and in Bangladesh, up to 500,000 lives were lost in one hurricane, in 1970. Each respective hurricane's storm surge was directly responsible for most of these deaths.

In the Indian Ocean from east Africa through Australia, tropical cyclones are known as CYCLONES or TROPICAL CYCLONES.

In the region from east of New Zealand to the west coast of South America, hurricanes are unlikely because ocean surface temperatures in that part of the South Pacific Ocean south of several degrees south latitude are not favorable for tropical storm development, and such storms do not form on or so close to the equator where the Coriolis force is zero or near zero.

e. hurricanes affecting Europe

Because, the Northern Hemisphere Atlantic Basin is smaller than the Northern Hemisphere Pacific Basin, it is more likely that a hurricane after recurving will infrequently survive across the ocean and strike Europe, than it is for a west Pacific typhoon to cross the Pacific to strike western North America.

For a tropical cyclone to move into western Europe as a hurricane, tropical storm or a hybrid tropical and extratropical low pressure system, one or more of the following must occur:

●the storm must recurve to the northeast while still in the central or eastern Atlantic;

●the storm must be very intense and/or very large;

●the storm must be moving fast (at 30 knots or more) so that it can cover a lot of territory quickly as it slowly loses tropical characteristics, and can move into Europe while still having at least some tropical identity;

●the storm must pass over the warm Gulf Stream for as long as possible;

●the sea-surface temperature over which it is passing is higher than normal; and

●no extratropical or other weather systems can act to shear off the storm's tops, which would act to diminish and subsequently dissolve the storm.

There may also be other factors that would help a hurricane to maintain its identity as it reaches western Europe, e.g., the storm passing through a strong theta-e ridge caused by a pooling of warm, moist air (theta-e is discussed in chapter 16).

Remnants of Atlantic hurricanes sometimes move into Europe. Some hurricanes make the transition from tropical to extratropical storm as they evolve from a warm-core system to a system with an upper-level low or trough, and move into the British Isles or Scandinavia with powerful gales.

It is interesting to look at some examples of hurricanes or hybrid storms that have hit Europe.

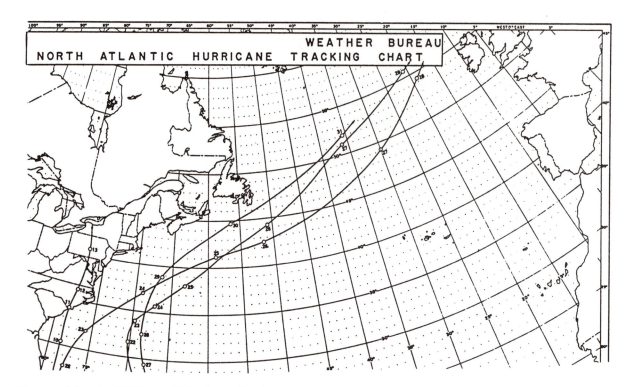

Figure 26. In 1883, well before there arose modern tracking technology, two hurricanes were plotted moving north of the British Isles. (source: NOAA)

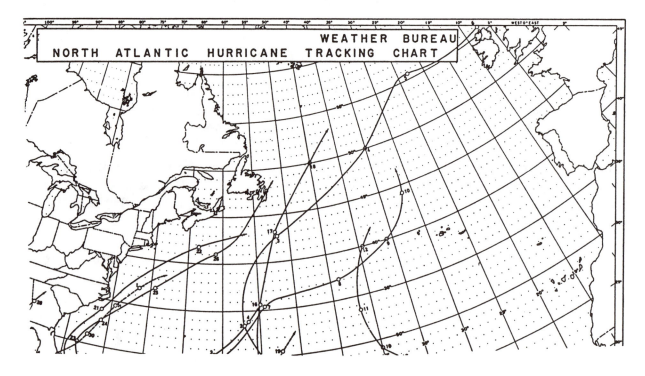

Figure 27. In 1887, this hurricane travelled to the north of Great Britain but sufficiently close to affect the area. (source: NOAA)

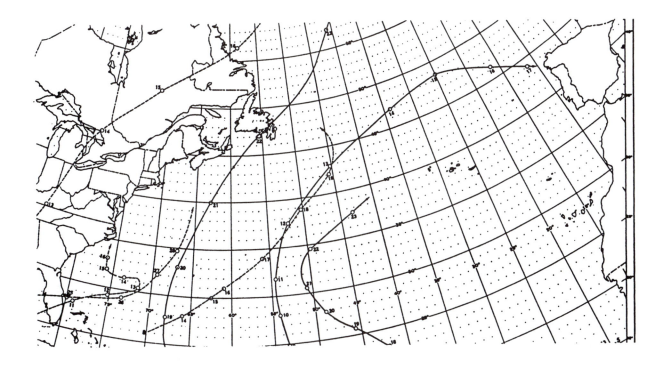

Figure 28. In 1892, a hurricane recurved in the middle Atlantic, and apparently lasted until almost moving inland at Spain and Portugal. (source: NOAA)

Figure 29. This 1906 tropical storm made a loop in the central Atlantic, subsequently becoming extra-tropical as it headed towards Wales.
(source: NOAA)

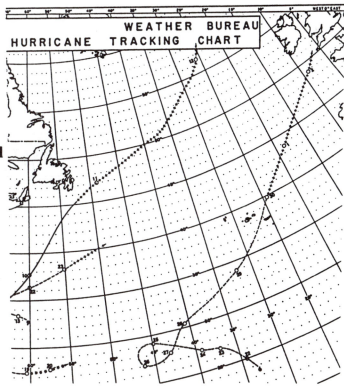

Figure 30. This tropical cyclone had a long path across the Atlantic in 1922 before expiring as a tropical system west of France. (source: NOAA)

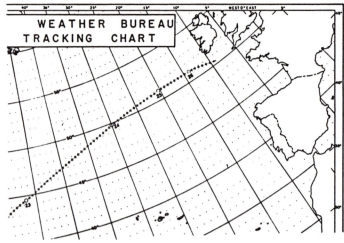

Figure 31. Apparently no hurricanes, tropical storms or hybrid storms moved into western Europe between 1922 and 1950. In 1950, Hurricane Dog (yes, that was the name given to it [see chapter 6, The Naming of Hurricanes]) skirted Ireland as a tropical storm on September 16th. (source: NOAA)

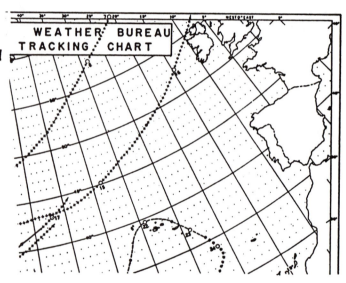

Figure 32. In 1953, two Hurricanes, Dolly on Sept. 17th and Edna three days later, moved toward Europe as tropical storms. Both storms formed in the eastern Caribbean Sea. Dolly expired before moving into Portugal, and Edna fizzled before reaching Ireland. (source: NOAA)

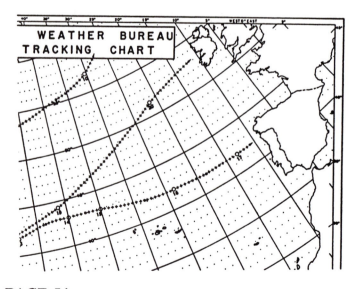

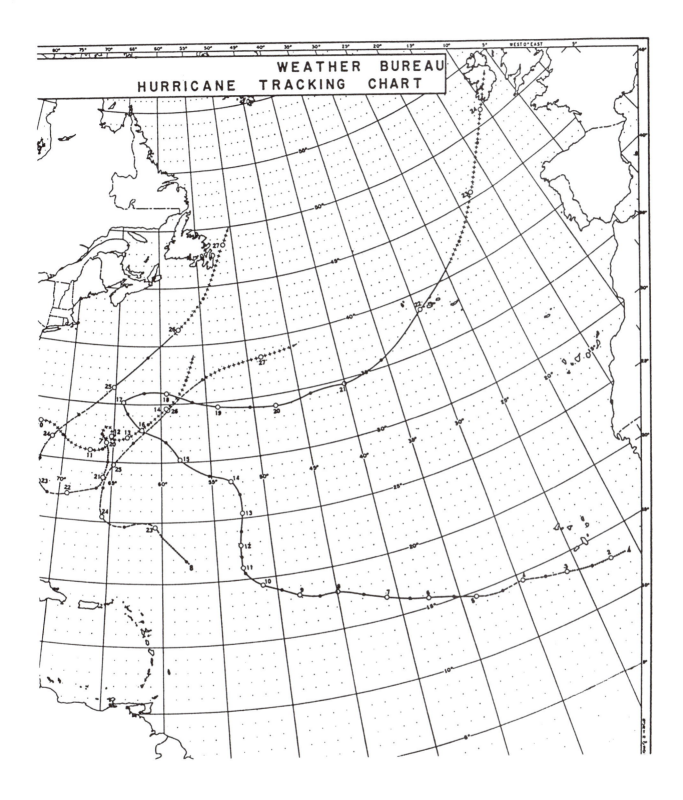

Figure 33. On September 24th, 1957, Hurricane Carrie did move ashore in Ireland as a tropical storm. (source: NOAA)

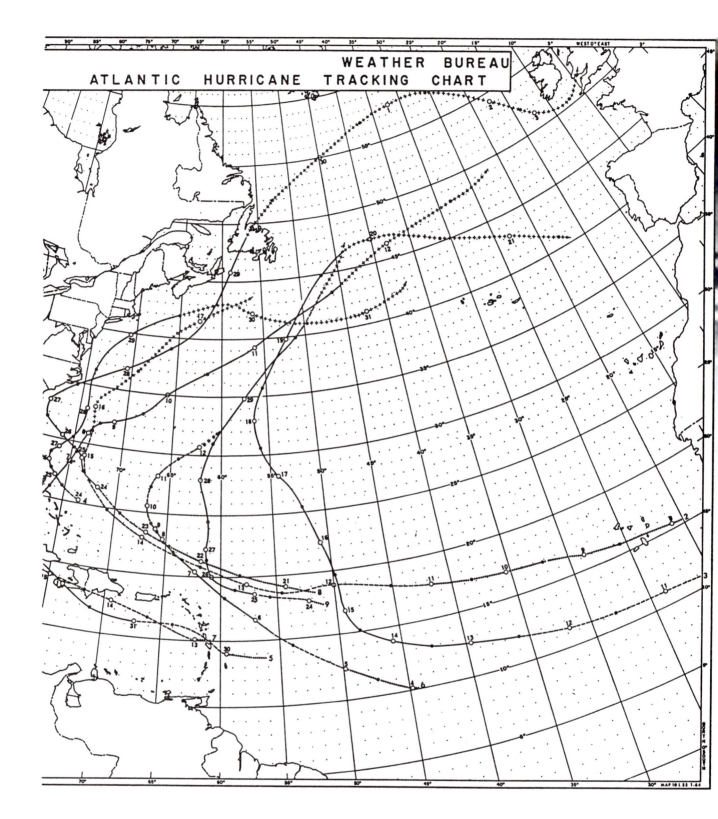

Figure 34. The following year, Hurricane Helene formed in the central Atlantic, brushed the Carolinas, smashed into Newfoundland, Canada as a hurricane, and moved across the Atlantic to enter Wales on October 3rd as a tropical storm. (source: NOAA)

Figure 35. Here is an example of a full-fledged hurricane striking Europe. Note that Debbie was first spotted as a hurricane in the Cape Verde Islands off Africa's west coast on Sept. 6th, 1961. Her path recurved well east of North America, in the mid-Atlantic, resulting in a direct hit as a hurricane on Ireland on the 15th and 16th. At that time, Debbie was moving quite fast, accelerating to about 50 miles in an hour, but maintaining full hurricane intensity as she moved into western Ireland. (source: NOAA)

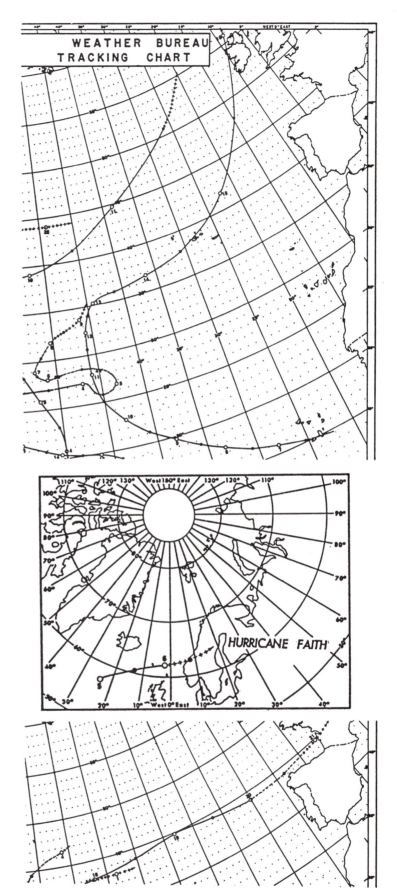

Figure 36. On September 6th, 1966, Hurricane Faith struck Norway as a tropical storm, just hours after diminishing from hurricane intensity. Faith continued as a tropical storm into Sweden. This storm may have arguably been becoming rapidly extratropical during this period; thus, by the time Faith reached Sweden, she was probably a hybrid storm. (source: NOAA)

Figure 37. On Sept. 21st, 1967, Hurricane Chloe had been down-graded for a day to a Tropical Storm when she moved into France. Chloe was, like Debbie of 1961, a Cape Verde Islands hurricane that recurved well before getting close to the U.S. east coast. (source: NOAA)

In October 1973, Hurricane Fran formed east of Florida, taking a path northeastward across the Atlantic. Some 350 miles west of the French coast on October 12th, Fran was still a hurricane, but then lost intensity rapidly, dying along the west coast of France.

In 1981, Hurricane Irene, forming southwest of the Cape Verde Islands, also died as she approached France on October 3rd, but did skirt Spain that day.

Thus, although hurricanes, tropical storms and hybrid storms are not common in western Europe, they do reach the shores of that continent occasionally. In modern weather records, however, it is rare to have a storm of categories 1 or 2 strength move into Europe, and category 3 or above hurricanes have never survived with such fury into Europe. Crossing colder waters and coming under influences of extratropical systems typically destroy tropical cyclones before they make it that far northeast.

MEDITERRANEAN SEA HURRICANES?

Another intriguing issue concerning hurricanes and Europe is this: Can hurricanes ever form over the warm Mediterranean Sea and move into southern Europe, southwest Asia or northern Africa?

Very infrequently, suspicious storms that look like tropical systems on satellite imagery and radar, will strike Europe's Mediterranean coast with powerful gales and torrential rainfall. Such storms occurred in September 1969, January 1982 and January 1995. The journal, Atmospheric Physics, Vol. 56, No. 4 for November 1983, contains an article by Billing, Haupt and Tonn entitled, "Evolution of a Hurricane-like Cyclone in the Mediterranean Sea".

Here is some documentation on the January 1995 storm.

During an oceanographic research cruise in the eastern Mediterranean, the vessel encountered winds in excess of hurricane intensity. Sustained winds hit 90 mph. The location was about 37°N to 38°N, 18°E. The satellite imagery showed an eye at the center of this storm.

This area, around Cyprus, is a region of cyclogenesis at that time of the year. However, in this particular storm, the temperature lapse rate was quite unstable, since the 500 mb (500 hPa) temperatures were around -36°C, which is colder than usual.

Was this indeed a hurricane, or perhaps a hurricane imbedded within a larger extratropical low pressure system, as happened off New England in an early 1990s "hurricane blizzard"?

The bottom line is this: since meteorologists, especially research meteorologists, will argue whether such systems are "tropical" or "extratropical" or perhaps a hybrid of both, what we are demonstrating is that there is yet much to learn about the evolution of storms.

f. arctic hurricanes

The various types of weather satellite imagery have enabled us to discover weather features that we never knew existed. For example, the following were "discovered", that is, defined, thanks to this imagery: thunderstorm outflow boundaries, mesoscale convective systems, and now, arctic hurricanes.

By definition, hurricanes are tropical cyclones, meaning that they form in either the tropics or, when they form just outside the tropics, that they form in tropical conditions. Therefore, when satellite imagery discovered that parts of the Arctic in the winter experience hurricanes, then these storms had to be given some other name, hence the term ARCTIC HURRICANE.

When they do strike land, the arctic hurricanes strike primarily Norway and Alaska. Indeed, the Norsemen of old wrote about encounters with some storms on the sea. Viking poets, called skalds, wrote about such encounters.

In the January-February 1991 issue of The American Scientist, Dr. Steven Businger documented the arctic hurricane, which he has been studying for many years. One of the most fascinating aspects of his studies include the following.

Satellite images of arctic hurricanes, such as of the one over the Bering Sea from March 7th and 8th, 1977, show a symmetrical spiralling cloud shield under about 180 miles in diameter (under 300 km diameter), with an eye...a clear eye...in the storm's center. Moreover, the clouds surrounding the eye were intense CUMULONIMBUS CLOUDS. The hurricane force winds are in a band and reach maximum intensity at low altitudes around the clear eye.

In the 1977 storm, National Weather Service observations from St. Paul Island, Alaska showed a sharp V signature on the barograph, which is what occurs when a hurricane passes over an observing site, and the temperature and dewpoint temperature had pronounced maxima as the arctic hurricane passed over. The storm had a warm core, which is what a hurricane has.

A Russian icebreaker in the western Bering Sea encountered 30-foot waves as it passed through the storm.

The arctic hurricane forms rapidly, is relatively small, and typically moves along the coastal waters off Norway and Alaska. It is sometimes not detected because of its small size, until it hits land but only if the arctic hurricane hits where there are people to observe the storm. Sometimes offshore oil rigs are the only inhabited areas to report these storms in the winter.

Therefore, the Arctic atmosphere is still in need of much research. The arctic hurricane has been only recently discovered, analogous to how thunderstorm outflow boundaries and mesoscale convective complexes were discovered not too long ago (MCSes were not truly defined until about 1979 and 1980).

Figure 38. An arctic hurricane with its spiral bands of cumulonimbus clouds, its clear eye, and its convective feeder bands, as shown in an infrared weather satellite image taken at 21Z (2100 Universale Temps Coordinée) March 8th, 1977.

The storm's diameter is about 300 kilometers (about 180 miles), which is small compared with tropical hurricanes. This arctic hurricane has just passed over St. Paul Island.

Infrared satellite imagery detects the temperature of the tops of clouds, or, if there are no clouds, the temperature of the land, sea or ice surface.

(source: NOAA, from NOAA-5 polar orbiter satellite)

The polar tropopause is much lower than the tropical tropopause, and in winter the tropopauses are at their lowest, while in summer the tropopauses are at their highest. For the benefit of non-weatherpeople reading this, the tropopause is the top of the troposphere and separates the troposphere from the stratosphere. The temperature typically falls as one ascends through the troposphere, but rises in the stratosphere due to absorption of some short-wave solar radiation by ozone that is created there. In the summer tropics, the tropopause averages about 50.000 to 60.000 feet high, and in the Arctic winter it is only about 20,000 feet high, sometimes lower.

The arctic hurricane grows rapidly as fluxes of heat from the sea-surface feed it. Arctic and tropical hurricanes occur at respectively different thermal regimes: the tropical cyclone occurring when tropical sea-surface temperatures are at a maximum, and the Arctic "arctic hurricane" occurring typically from November through March.

The logical question is, "How could a hurricane form in the Arctic during the dead of winter?"

Relatively warm air is lifted over descending cold air, but the environment is unstable. The temperature cools off rapidly as one ascends through the Arctic troposphere, such that rising air parcels, which cool at a specified rate when unsaturated and at a less rapid pace when saturated due to the release of the heat of condensation when saturated parcels are forced to rise farther, will be positively buoyant, i.e., will keep rising, forming cumulonimbus clouds, which are convective clouds.

The arctic hurricane tends to form over Arctic ocean areas in which the warm ocean water meets the winter ice pack.

Good documentation of another arctic hurricane was done by Norwegian scientists over the Norwegian Sea in a February 1984 storm. Thus, a small army of weather investigators is trying to discover the mysteries of the arctic hurricane. As of this writing, there is no intensive search underway for these polar hurricanes in the Antarctic.

4. THE STRUCTURE OF A HURRICANE

a. basic definitions

TROPICAL DISTURBANCE, TROPICAL WAVE - A tropical disturbance or tropical wave is a discrete system of organized convection that has a no fronts associated with it and is migratory, maintaining its identity for 24 hours or longer. It forms in the tropics, or, when forming just outside the tropics, in tropical conditions.

MESOSCALE CONVECTIVE SYSTEM (MCS) - An MCS is a relatively large area (150 or more miles - 250 or more kilometers - in average diameter) of organized thunderstorms that persists for at least 15 hours. A tropical disturbance can originate as an MC, e.g., when it forms over equatorial Africa and then moves into the Atlantic Ocean to become the tropical disturbance.

EASTERLY WAVE - An easterly wave is a type of tropical disturbance that moves generally westward, steered by the tropical easterly winds, and appears on the surface weather map as an inverted trough.

WEST AFRICAN DISTURBANCE LINE (WADL) - A WADL is a line of convection averaging about 300 miles - 480 kilometers - long, and is similar to a squall line. It forms over west Africa north of the equator and south of 15°N latitude and can be a seedling for a tropical storm if it moves out over the Atlantic Ocean.

INTERTROPICAL CONVERGENCE ZONE (ITCZ) - The ITCZ is a region of converging, rising air with its axis meandering typically from several degrees north of the equator to 10 or somewhat more degrees north of the equator. It is forced by the Northern Hemisphere tropics northeasterly prevailing low-level winds, and Southern Hemisphere tropics southeasterly prevailing low-level winds. The clockwise circulation around high pressure systems in the Northern Hemisphere Atlantic and Pacific Oceans, and the counterclockwise circulation around similar high prressure systems in the Southern Hemisphere during the Northern Hemisphere's hurricane season, create the low-level wind pattern and consequent convergence that result in the Intertropical Convergence Zone.

TROPICAL CYCLONE - A tropical cyclone is the generic name for tropical storms, hurricanes and typhoons. It is a warm-core low pressure system with no fronts, that develops over tropical waters or, when just outside the tropics, over waters in tropical conditions, and has an organized circulation.

TROPICAL DEPRESSION - A tropical depression is a tropical cyclone in which the maximum sustained surface winds (a one-minute average) are 38 miles per hour (33 knots) or less.

TROPICAL STORM - A tropical storm is a warm-core tropical cyclone in which the maximum sustained surface winds range from 39 to 73 miles per hour (34 to 63 knots).

HURRICANE - A hurricane is a warm-core tropical cyclone in which the maximum sustained surface winds are 74 miles per hour (64 knots) or greater.

EYE-WALL - The eye-wall is an organized band of convection that immediately surrounds the center (eye) of a tropical cyclone. The fiercest winds and most intense rainfall typically occur near the eye-wall.

EYE - The typically clear or mostly clear center of a mature hurricane. The winds are light or nearly calm. The eye typically appears when the tropical storm achieves hurricane status - about 74 mph.

b. outer-hurricane squall-line

Figure 39 on the next page shows a radar composite of the many hurricanes, illustrating a composite average of many hurricanes. No one hurricane necessarily looks exactly like this, but most hurricanes appear like this composite, so that we can use it to conceptualize what the structure of most hurricanes looks like.

When a hurricane is moving towards you, the first weather element you will likely observe is the appearance of high-level clouds on the storm's periphery. These are the cirrus and cirrostratus clouds, which subsequently lower and thicken into the middle-level clouds and then low-level clouds as the storm approaches.

Then, there often exists an outer-hurricane squall line at the leading edge of the storm relative to how the storm is moving. This is a gusty line of showers and thunderstorms and may be a broken line rather than a solid one. The wave heights should also begin increasing.

The pre-hurricane squall line is typically fairly straight. It does not have the spiral pattern which is to follow when the outer convective bands move in. The pre-hurricane squall line is as much as 50 or more miles out ahead of the first ragged rainfall areas of the hurricane's outer bands.

The line is typically about 100 to 200 miles ahead of the eye, but in very large hurricanes, has been observed on radar to occur as much as some 500 miles ahead of the hurricane's eye.

Bursts of showery rain and some gusty winds occur when the line passes through, but winds are not particularly strong.

The first significant wind and rain from the hurricane is next, as the fist of the outer convective spiral bands moves in.

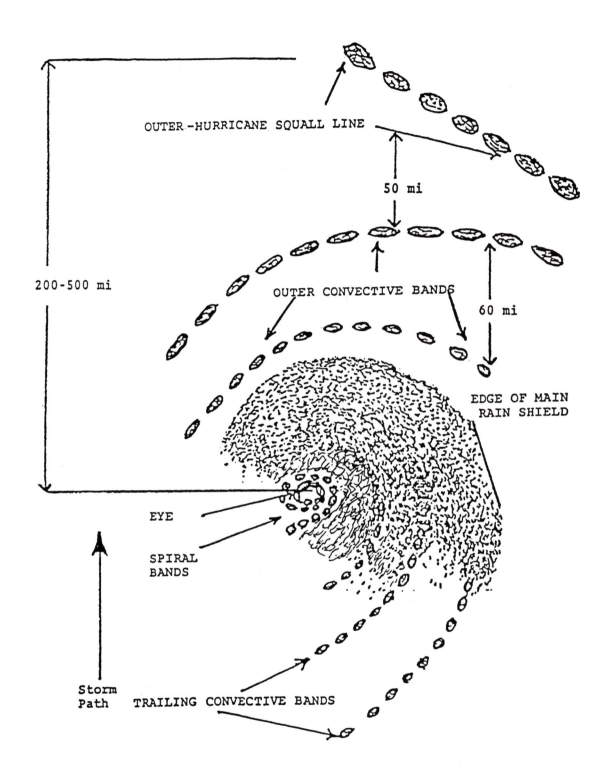

OUTER-HURRICANE SQUALL LINE

50 mi

200-500 mi

OUTER CONVECTIVE BANDS

60 mi

EDGE OF MAIN
RAIN SHIELD

EYE

SPIRAL
BANDS

Storm
Path   TRAILING CONVECTIVE BANDS

Figure 39. Above is a composite average of many hurricanes, based on many years of looking at radar images of hurricanes. The shaded-in sections are areas of rainfall. There may be more outer convective spiral bands than indicated in the diagram.

PAGE 64

c. outer convective bands

A hurricane typically has two to five outer convective bands, which are comprised of thunderstorm and shower cells. These bands are before the main rain shield moves in. Each successive convective band closer to the eye may contain progressively stronger wind gusts, especially if the hurricane contains more than two of these spiral bands.

The term convective means relating to convection, that is, to cumuloform clouds that grow into showers and thunderstorms.

The outer convective bands are typically from 40 to 80 miles...65 to 130 kilometers...apart, and in large hurricanes the outermost one can be as much as some 300 miles...480 kilometers...out from the eye.

d. rain shield

After the passage of the last outer convective band, the next part of the hurricane to arrive is the solid or nearly-solid rain shield. The rain typically become progressively heavier and the wind steadily increases as the eye approaches. When the sustained winds reach 39 mph, the tropical-storm-force wind threshold has been reached. When the sustained winds reach 74 mph, the hurricane-force threshold has been reached. There are gusts that are higher than the sustained wind. When hurricane conditions are occurring, the gust can be 30 mph or somewhat higher than the sustained windspeed. For example, it is common for a category four hurricane with sustained winds 150 mph to be producing gusts of 175 to 180 mph or even somewhat more.

Because of the intense winds, the rainfall is difficult to measure. Since much of the precipitation occurring with the rain shield is blowing horizontally, some estimates indicate that perhaps a considerable amount of the rain may not be caught by every rain gauge in the affected area. Even so, radar and satellite estimates of rainfall in hurricanes easily justify five to ten inch rainfalls in even a minor hurricane, and considerably more in a powerful and large system. Exacerbating the excessive rainfall threat is a hurricane with a slow movement...one advancing at no more than ten miles per hour. Rainfalls of over fifteen inches from a hurricane are not unusual. In an extreme example, Hurricane Easy deluged Yankeetown, Florida on September 5th, 1950 with a torrential rainfall of about forty inches in a 24-hour period. Thus, most of the hurricane's rainfall occurs in the usually-solid rain shield.

The rain shield typically surrounds the eye in a well-developed hurricane, and as its outer edge moves in over your area, you observe that the leading edge is usually well-defined.

e. eye-wall

The region of intense convection that surrounds the hurricane's eye is called the eye-wall. It may be vertical or slanted around the eye. Within the eye-wall is where the most intense windspeeds are observed...the hurricane's maximum sustained winds. The eye-wall also usually produces the most intense rainfall.

The eye-wall often appears to contain straight-line segments along its inner-edge, forming a changing polygon as parts of the segments grow and others die, to be replaced by new ones. This is why hurricanes sometimes appear on radar to be wobbling rather than taking a smooth straight or curved path, i.e., the ever-changing line segments of the inner-edge of the eye-wall "relocates" the eye perhaps a mile or more to the left or right of its average path from hour to hour.

Within the rain shield and eye-wall, an observer can often find either spiral-shaped rain and wind patterns, if a hurricane is asymmetrical (a weak or minimal hurricane), or the observer can often find ringlike regions of very active convective heat release surrounding the eye, if a hurricane is symmetrical, which would be in a strong hurricane.

The spiral bands curve counterclockwisely in the Northern Hemisphere, and clockwisely in the Southern Hemisphere, inward toward the center of the storm and seemingly merge to form the eye-wall that surrounds the eye. These bands can be fairly wide, but become narrow near the eye.

A more-steady stratiform rain occurs between convective spiral bands.

When the storm is moving inland, hurricane tornadoes, when they are spawned, seem to occur chiefly in these convective rings or bands that feed into the hurricane.

f. eye of the hurricane

The cyclonic circulation around the center of the hurricane is comprised of the air spiraling in towards the center but also rising. At the center of low pressure the eye does not appear until the winds reach about hurricane strength. A study by two researchers, L. Shapiro and H. Willoughby, found that in most cases, the eye of the hurricane first appears when the maximum sustained tangential wind speed exceeds about 78 mph.

The eye of a hurricane is typically quasi-circular or quasi-oval, tending to be more circular in the more intense storms. The winds are light and the skies are clear to partly cloudy, and typically free of rain. The sun shines in the daytime as the eye passes over.

Figure 40. A weather satellite image of Hurricane Diana at 2030Z September 11th, 1984. Note that the eye is located just off the North Carolina coast. This is a well-defined eye for a symmetrical organized hurricane. Note also the feeder bands from over the Atlantic into the storm. These are bands of energy, in the form of warm, moist air, which sustain the storm. There is also anticyclonic (clockwise in the Northern Hemisphere) outflow aloft in the top levels of the hurricane. (source: NOAA)

Sometimes entire flocks of birds that got trapped in the storm will fly with the eye for sanctuary.

Once you are in the rain shield as the hurricane moves in, the wind and rain gradually intensify as the eye approaches. You are experiencing the greatest fury of the wind when suddenly the eye-wall passes and the wind drops to nearly nothing. The sun usually comes out, or if the hurricane is passing over at night, you usually see the stars. Then, after the eye passes, the full fury of the winds strike suddenly as the eye-wall on the other side passes over. Subsequently, with the hurricane's center moving away, the wind and rain gradually subside, in opposite progression to what occurred as the eye approached.

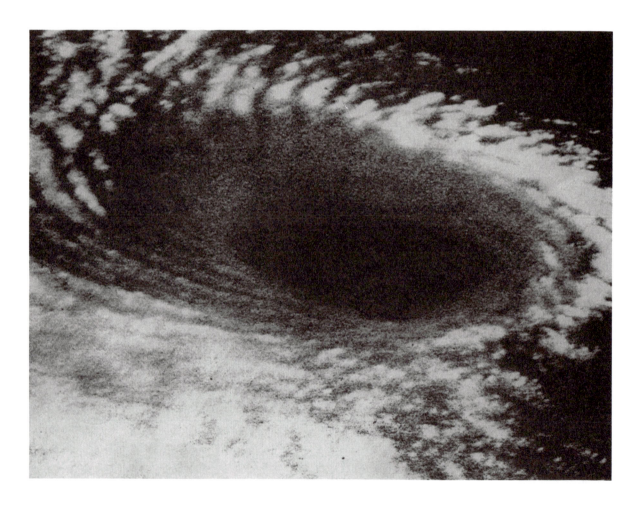

Figure 41. The eye of Hurricane Irah, Sept. 24th, 1973, as photographed by the space station Skylab. (source: NASA)

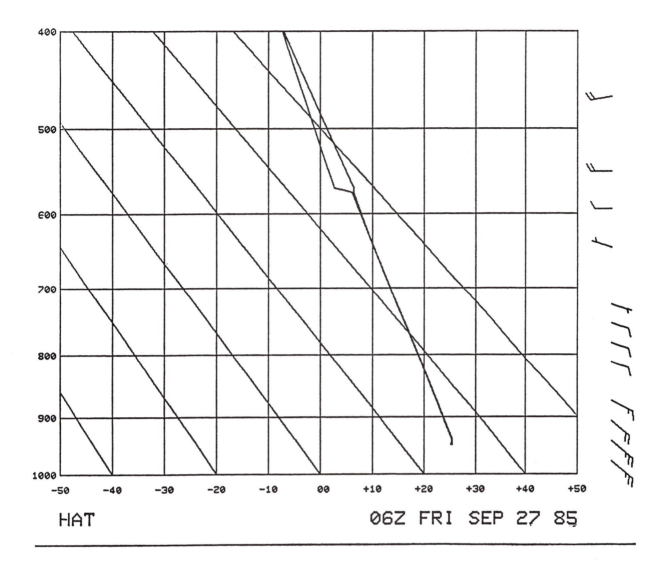

Figure 42. Above is the thermodynamic vertical sounding of temperature, dewpoint and wind as taken by a weather balloon launched into the eye of Hurricane Gloria when she was passing directly over Cape Hatteras, North Carolina at 06Z Sept. 27th, 1985. The +y ordinate is the pressure level in millibars (hectoPascals), and the +x abscissa is the temperature in degrees Celsius. The plot is the temperature curve and, to its left, the dewpoint temperature curve. Note that the air is saturated, with the temperature and dewpoint curves on top of each other, from the surface to about the 575 millibar level. Most winds, even in the vertical, are under 20 knots. Wind barbs are plotted to the right. Even though the eye was essentially clear, the air was quite moist. (source: NWS)

Although the air rises to condense and form the clouds and subsequent precipitation as it spirals within the hurricane around the eye, the air sinks and warms as it does so, inside the eye.

The average diameter of the eye of a hurricane is from 20 to 30 miles. However, eyes have been observed to be as large as 50 miles across, with the extreme example being about 100 miles. When Hurricane Donna was passing New York City on Sept. 12th, 1960 with 100+ mph winds, the western edge of the eye was just off the Staten Island shore and the eastern edge was south of eastern Long Island. Donna may have been one of those hurricanes with a double-eye, one off Staten Island and the other eye south of Suffolk County, Long Island. However, it is arguable whether it is physically possible for a hurricane to have more than one eye, since it is expected to have one center of circulation.

The smallest eyes have been from 5 to 10 miles across, with an eye as small as 5 to 7 miles being unusual.

As a hurricane "spins-up" or intensifies, the swirl of air circulating around the eye causes the eye to shrink. Therefore, one sign that a hurricane is undergoing intensification is the shrinking in size of its eye. An excellent example occurred on October 4th, 1995 in Hurricane Opal in the Gulf of Mexico. After leaving the Yucatan Peninsula as a strong and large tropical depression, the system emerged over 80=degree F. water north of Yucatan and strengthened into a tropical storm. Later, as the system moved north-northeastward over water with surface temperatures of 86°F or higher, it intensified rapidly, becoming a hurricane with 150 mph sustained winds. This was by late morning on October 4th, which is when the hurricane hunters found when they flew into Opal, that the eye shrunk rapidly to only 7 miles in diameter.

The eyewall contraction cannot get to be much more. What also happens is that a new eyewall may form inside the old one and move outward, or a new eyewall may form outside the old one and move inward. When this happens, intensity changes typically occur. Recall that the eye-wall is comprised of discrete lines of convection, so that in essence we have a polygon when we inspect the eye's lining in very fine detail. The circular or oval eye is ringed not by a truly circular or truly oval eye-wall, but by an eye-wall made up of individual fairly-straight short segments of convection, each segment of which grows and dies, replaced by a new segment when it dies.

Indeed, when a hurricane's eye shrinks to below ten miles because it has spun up into a powerful storm, perhaps a superhurricane (a large category 5 storm), the eyewall decontracts...that is to say, a hurricane does not maintain such a small eye for a long period of time...up to 24 hours may be the typical maximum for an eye only 5 to 7 miles across.

Thus, hurricanes have eye-wall cycles.

The eye in Opal expanded and the hurricane diminished some in intensity before striking the Florida panhandle near Pensacola later that evening, with the highest sustained winds dropping from 150 mph to 125 mph. The peak gust reported near the eye on land was 144 mph.

Hurricane eyes typically like to stay in the range of about 20 to 30 miles in diameter.

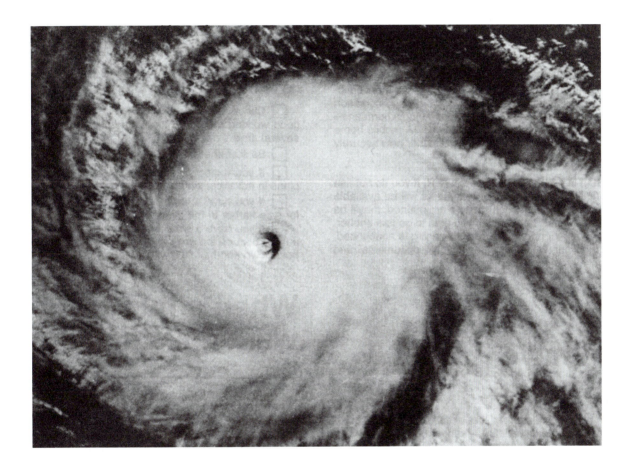

Figure 43. The clouds of a well-organized hurricane with an eye of from 20 to 30 miles in diameter. The outer convective bands are followed by the rain shield, then the eye-wall and the eye, as the hurricane moves in. The process is reversed as the hurricane's center moves away from the observer. (source: NOAA)

Figure 44. At left, the fierce winds and intense rainfall during the height of the hurricane just before reaching the eye-wall; at right, the eye-wall passes and you enter the eye of the hurricane, with light wind and mostly clear skies. (source: NOAA)

Figure 45. A radar presentation of part of a hurricane. The white areas are precipitation. Note the precipitation-free area just below the middle of the radar screen: this is the eye of the hurricane. The center of the screen is the location of the weather station. Each concentric ring on the scope represents a range of 25 miles. The outermost circle is 125 miles out from the radar site. (source: NOAA)

Figure 46. A rare radar image of a double concentric eye in a hurricane. This picture is from the weather office in Madras, India in a 1990 tropical cyclone. Note the eye and the eye-wall of precipitation surrounding it, followed by another mostly precipitation-free (dark) ring. (source: Indian Meteorological Division)

The above hurricane moved into India in 1990. Once in a while in a hurricane, as in this example, a concentrated ring of convection will develop outside the eye-wall. When this has been observed, the phenomenon has occurred in symmetrical mature hurricanes.

The ring propagates inwards, forming a double-eye. This is not the same as "two eyes"; this is one "double-eye". The inner eye-wall then dissipates as the outer one intensifies and then it moves inward. This same cycle occurred three times in Superhurricane Allen in 1980.

As the outer concentrated ring of convection is moving inward and intensifying, the eye-wall often diminishes in intensity. At some point in the evolution of the new eye-wall, the strongest winds and the heaviest rains occur in the outer convective ring.

Such concentric rings are most likely in intense hurricanes...categories 4 and 5. When such rings occur, they usually signal the termination of a period of intensification. Such hurricanes then maintain quasi-constant intensity or then weaken. When the inner eye completely dissipates, then we may see more intensification.

Hurricane Frederic in 1979 and Hurricane Gert in 1981 each had a asymmetrical double-eye, rather than a symmetrical double-eye. These double-eyes were comprised of spiral bands which partially encircled the eyes, rather than being comprised of convective rings.

Figure 47. Hurricane Edna of 1954 had two eyes for a time. The paths of Carol and Edna are shown, with the dots showing eye positions at 7 a.m. EDT. These storms occurred less than two weeks apart. Hurricane Dolly, which occurred between Carol and Edna, veered out to sea off the Carolinas. Otherwise, the mid-Atlantic and northeast states would have been struck by three hurricanes in less than two weeks. Hurricane Hazel ravaged much of the same area in October. The following year, Hurricanes Connie and Diane struck the same general area within one week of each other. Then Hurricane Ione struck North Carolina. Thus, the same area of the east coast has been hit by multiple hurricanes in consecutive years. (source: NWS)

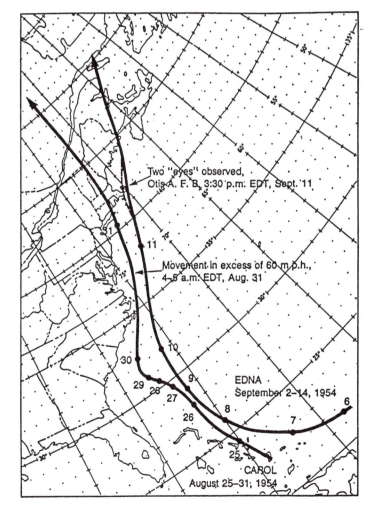

g. feeder bands

Let us look again at well-organized, symmetrical Superhurricane Allen of 1980, in figure 48 on the next page.

Note the bands of clouds spiralling in towards the center of the hurricane. These are the feeder bands which supply much of the energy of the hurricane.

The hurricane grows and sustains itself for as long as the environment through which it is passing is favorable. The sea-surface temperature must be at least 79°F...26°C. When these water temperatures are at least 86°F, as happens in summer and early autumn in parts of the Gulf of Mexico, then the storm can grow rapidly in size and strength. Moreover, some other weather system must not be generating a strong wind shear aloft, above about 18,000 feet up, that can shear off the tops of the tropical cyclone. For example, if a strong extratropical trough of low pressure were generating a southwest wind of 60 knots at the 18,000-foot level (which is about the 500 millibar pressure level), and these winds increased to over 100 knots at the 35,000-foot level (about 250 millibars), with the hurricane heading westward into the trough, then these strong southwesterly winds would rapidly "blow off" the top of the hurricane, weakening or dissipating it, and disturbing its vertical motion pattern. Moreover, the trough would likely steer the westward-moving hurricane to the northeast. A strong trough, though with winds not as strong as in our example, remained over the U.S. east coast during the first half of the very active 1995 hurricane season, and saved the east coast from being hit by a series of hurricanes forming in the Atlantic Basin in conveyor-like fashion.

Returning to our discussion on the feeder bands, evaporation of some very warm surface water provides the warm, moist air which contains much of the energy potential for hurricane development. As this air rises into the storm, it cools to its dewpoint forming clouds and as it keeps rising, cloud droplets coalesce and accrete to form the raindrops. In this condensation process, the "heat of condensation" is released. This is a form of energy. The hurricane uses this energy to maintain itself and grow.

When the temperature and dewpoint are high, as over the tropical waters, the energy available is enormous. One study concluded that the amount of energy expended by a typical hurricane would, if it could be harnessed, supply the entire energy needs for the United States for half a year.

If a hurricane is moving up the coast just inland, the feeder bands from over the ocean would help sustain the storm longer than if the storm were well inland and lost contact with its chief source of energy. If the storm maintains its circulation and reemerges over warm sea-water, it can reintensify.

Figure 48. Looking again at Hurricane Allen of 1980, with his eye just off the tip of Yucatan. Notice the feeder bands of energy spiraling into the hurricane, towards its center. (source: NOAA)

h. air circulation in a hurricane

Air spirals into the hurricane, rising as it does so, encircling the relatively calm eye. In the eye, the air is sinking, warming adiabatically as it descends. Although the perfect model of the circulation and energy evolutions of a tropical cyclone has not been formulated, we do have sufficient observations and data to suggest some circulation models of the storm.

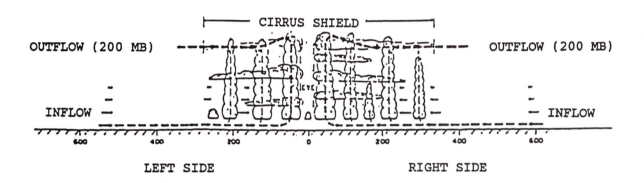

Figure 49. This is an idealized view of the mean radial circulation of air in a hurricane. This model does not account for the recycling of the air.

A more comprehensive model, as given on the next page, shows a higher degree of vertical exchange of energy, moisture and momentum. The smaller-scale, called mesoscale, features within the hurricane need to be displayed. For example, not all hurricanes should be expected to have vertical eye-walls. Indeed, one study of five hurricanes found that their eye-walls leaned outward, which would suggest a sloping updraft.

Some of the details that a comprehensive hurricane circulation model should account for are:
- the maintenance of the hurricane's convection;
- the lifting of evaporated water out of the planetary boundary layer;
- the greater tapping of the ocean energy source through downdraft drying and cooling of the boundary layer; and
- the balancing of the hurricane's circulation against radiational cooling.

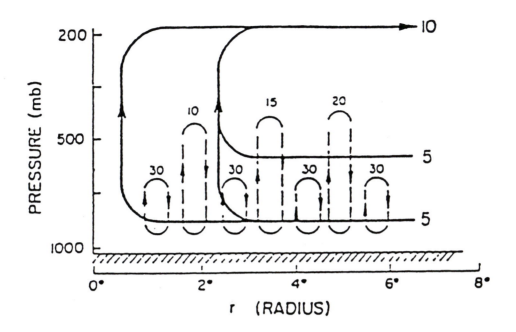

Figure 50. This idealized cross-section of a hurricane's mean radial circulation is superimposed with the recycling of the air (mass recycling). The numbers on these units are arbitrary and represent the mass transport. The radius values are in degrees of latitude. (source: after W. Gray)

i. anticyclonic outflow aloft

The air does not just keep spiralling in counterclockwise in the Northern Hemisphere and clockwise in the Southern Hemisphere, and disappearing. Due to conservation of mass, the air has to go somewhere to maintain a circulation. Aloft in the hurricane, towards and at and over its top, the air comes out in an anticyclonic (clockwise in the Northern Hemisphere and counterclockwise in the Southern Hemisphere) fashion. Thus, a hurricane moving across the Atlantic towards the United States, and a typhoon heading across the western Pacific towards Japan, and a tropical cyclone heading across the Indian Ocean towards India, all have, since they are Northern Hemisphere tropical cyclones, a counterclockwise cyclonic circulation with an anticyclonic outflow aloft. This outflow is hard to distinguish on individual weather satellite pictures, but on time-lapse video-loops of these pictures you can detect a surge of high cirroform clouds spiralling clockwise aloft out of the storm.

PAGE 77

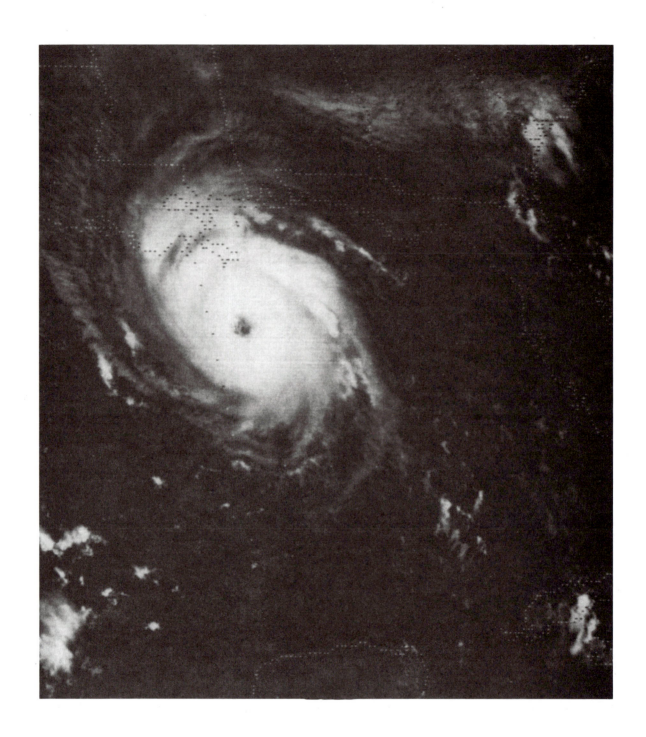

Figure 51. A visible satellite picture of Hurricane Andrew in August of 1992, after he raked south Florida and approached the Gulf Coast. The mostly clear eye is easily visible, some feeder bands exist, and to the north aloft some of the clouds are high cirroform clouds which are part of the anticyclonic outflow aloft of the hurricane. (source: NOAA)

A strong anticyclonic outflow from a powerful hurricane can kill a weaker storm that just happens to be nearby. For example, in September 1989, when massive category 4 Hurricane Hugo was moving away from Puerto Rico towards South Carolina, its anticyclonic outflow aloft was so strong and extensive that it slashed across the top of Tropical Storm Iris, which had been intensifying only a few hundred miles to Hugo's southeast. This intersection sheared the upper portion of Iris and destroyed her.

In August 1995, Hurricane Humberto did the same to another Tropical Storm named Iris. It just seems hard for a storm named Iris to get its eye together.

The cloud tops of hurricanes average about 50,000 feet, with the anticyclonic outflow probably occurring chiefly in the top 20,000 feet. This figure is subject to modification as we research this aspect of hurricanes better.

5. THE LIFE-CYCLE OF A HURRICANE

a. the incipient or seedling stage

A tropical storm forms from a tropical disturbance known as a SEEDLING. A tropical disturbance is a region of organized convection, which makes it readily apparent on an enhanced infrared weather satellite image because the coldest (highest) tops are readily detectable. Infrared images are images which show the temperatures of the targets, which in this case would show the temperatures of the cloud tops. The colder the cumulonimbus cloud tops with their cirrostratus tops, the higher they are. Inotherwords, deep convection is looked for.

Moreover, the disturbance begins to develop its own wind field, so that it perturbs the wind field through which it is passing.

Thus, a seedling is a tropical disturbance of organized convection that is associated with a perturbed wind field.

As we shall see in a later discussion in this book, these seedlings require the presence of warm, moist air, which is known as a high value of equivalent potential temperature, called "THETA-E" (described in chapter 16).

Over the Atlantic Basin, which includes the Caribbean Sea and Gulf of Mexico, and over Africa, there is a total of some one hundred seedlings forming during the hurricane season...essentially from around June 1st to November 15th. Most of these 100 or so seedlings originate over equatorial Africa and move out into the eastern North Atlantic.

Tropical disturbances take various forms: an easterly wave, a West African Disturbance Line (WADL), forming in a trough or starting out under an old cold low in the upper troposphere, or forming along an old polar front.

EASTERLY WAVE: An easterly wave is a tropical disturbance taking the shape of an inverted trough on the low-level weather maps, and moves in the tropics from generally east to west, steered by the tropical easterly winds.

Most of the seedlings are easterly waves. One study found that many if not most of the easterly waves begin as an area of instability in the easterly flow neat 10°N latitude in east or central Africa. Most last for several days and have a wavelength of about 1500 miles...2400 kilometers. Their average speed of westward progression is about 16 to 18 mph. Some easterly waves cross Central America into the Pacific Ocean.

Some easterly waves develop in the Intertropical Convergence Zone (ITCZ) (discussed earlier) and move westward within the ITCZ. Recall that the ITCZ is the Trade Winds confluence zone that exists in the Atlantic just north of the equator. In the Pacific, the

ITCZ is just north of the equator in the Northern Hemisphere summer, and just south of it in the Southern Hemisphere summer.

One study found that the North Atlantic has from about 50 to 80 easterly waves a year. Thus, out of the some 100 seedlings for hurricanes per year, some 50 to 80 of them are easterly waves.

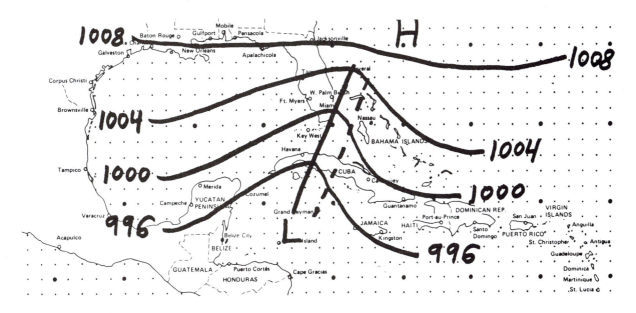

Figure 52. Here is an easterly wave on a surface weather map. The easterly wave is an inverted trough with the low-level convergence and its associated convective weather occurring on the east side of the wave axis.

When an easterly wave approaches from the east, the barometric pressure falls but the weather remains generally good; however, as the trough axis passes and the pressure rises, the convective precipitation...the showers and thunderstorms...occur. Recent studies have found that in the formative stage of the easterly wave over Africa, or over the eastern Atlantic when they first form there, the clouds and convection are on the west side of the trough axis.

WEST AFRICAN DISTURBANCE LINE (WADL): Some tropical cyclone seedlings originate as West African Disturbance Lines. A WADL is not an easterly wave, but is a line of convection about 300 miles...480 kilometers...long, similar to a squall line, which forms over west Africa north of the equator and south of about 15°N latitude.

There is a strong sinking and air and low-level divergence ahead of the WADL, which identifies the system readily because its leading edge is sharp. That is to say, the leading edge of the WADL is a line of thunderstorms, similar to what we expect in a well-organized squall line.

The WADL moves at from 20 to 40 mph. Compare that with the average easterly wave movement of some 16 to 18 mph. Like the easterly wave, the WADL moves essentially westward. The greatest area of convergence in a WADL is in the mid-troposphere along the disturbance line.

A new WADL forms over West Africa and moves into the Atlantic about every 4 to 5 days, mainly in the summer. Thus, there are typically about 30 of them during primarily the summer, that can function as tropical cyclone seedlings. Some WADLs reach the American tropics, out of which a few develop into tropical cyclones. Often, WADLs are thrown into the grouping identified as easterly waves, but there is a certain distinction between an easterly wave and a West African Disturbance Line.

DISTURBANCES IN THE INTERTROPICAL CONVERGENCE ZONE: One study found that about one-fourth of all tropical disturbances originate in the ITCZ. In that region, the low-level pressure gradient is weak and the Coriolis Force is very weak. Thus, these weak areas of low pressure are too close to the equator to develop a decent cyclonic circulation. However, when they reach to or form around 4 to 5 degrees of latitude north of the equator, then they have a fighting chance to develop a circulation, which gives them a chance to grow into a tropical cyclone.

TROUGH OR COLD LOW IN THE UPPER TROPOSPHERE: Only a few seedlings form when a cold cut-off low around 200 millibars up, or when an upper-level trough, extends from the mid-latitudes into the tropics. One study found that about 14% of the cut-off lows develop near Cape Hatteras, North Carolina and persist for up to two weeks. When a surface low develops under it over warm water, it eventually transforms into a warm-core system as the upper low or upper trough dissipates, and the development of a tropical cyclone occurs.

OLD POLAR FRONT: Tropical cyclones do not have fronts, although later in their paths as they move away from the tropics they often hook up with fronts as they die or transform into hybrid and then extratropical low pressure systems. However, the remnants of an old polar front that works its way to say the Gulf states or to the latitude of Florida and persists for several days, is a zone of convergence which, as it stays over warm water, can initiate a tropical disturbance. An MCS can form along or near the front, which can then evolve into a tropical cyclone.

b. the tropical storm stage

The circulation within a seedling gets stronger as the tropical disturbance feeds on warm, moist air over the tropical waters. The rising air into the system releases its heat of condensation which supplies much of the energy to the system for further intensification. Sustained winds of 15 to 35 mph are typically occurring as the system spins up. At this time, the system is labelled a **TROPICAL DEPRESSION.**

The system grows into a tropical storm as long as it remains over water that has a surface temperature of typically at least 79°F...26°C., and is not being sheared in mid and/or upper levels by another weather system. Water temperatures in the middle 80s F. or warmer, without the wind-shear inhibitor, almost ensure development.

Early-season tropical storms tend to form in the Gulf of Mexico and western Caribbean, and as the hurricane season progresses through July, the later storms tend to form in the Atlantic, with the formation area for the majority of them shifting eastward towards the African coast through August and September. This does not imply that tropical storms will not form in the Gulf or Caribbean late in season; for example, Opal and Roxanne formed in this area late in the 1995 hurricane season.

In fact, the main formation area seems to shift back to the western Caribbean Sea late in the hurricane season.

When the tropical depression with its closed circulation spins up to having sustained winds of 34 knots...39 miles per hour...it is classified a tropical storm and given a name. When the storm keeps strengthening, its sustained wind increase along with the peak gusts. For example, a tropical storm with a sustained (one-minute average) wind of 60 miles per hour would likely have gusts to at least 75 mph, which is hurricane strength. However, the storm is not classified as a hurricane until the SUSTAINED winds reach the threshold for hurricane force: 74 m.p.h....64 knots.

The tropical storm does not have an eye. It has its center of lowest pressure, but the eye does not form until the winds reach about or just above minimal hurricane intensity. This makes identification and classification readily allowable from looking at the system via satellite imagery. If it has an eye, it is a hurricane. If it does not have a discernable eye, it may be that the eye has temporarily filled with cloud matter or the storm is diminishing, but it still may be a hurricane. In general, however, a well-organized hurricane has an eye. A tropical cyclone of tropical storm intensity never has an eye.

Our definition, therefore, of a tropical storm is: a tropical storm is a warm-core tropical cyclone in which the maximum sustained surface winds range from 39 to 73 mph.

In the Atlantic Basin, out of some 100 seedlings each hurricane season, about ten become tropical storms, out of which about 6 become full-fledged hurricanes.

Some years have fewer tropical storms and hurricanes, while others have more. The 21 tropical storms and hurricanes reported in 1933 was likely a number lower than reality, because 1933 was well before weather radar (1957) and weather satellites (1960), so that tropical cyclones far at sea were reported only if a ship happened to pass through one. Now, all such systems are detected. Therefore, **weather records for tropical cyclone frequency should be considered accurate from the 1960 season through now.**

Whereas the average in the North Atlantic Basin is about 10 tropical storms and hurricanes, the annual average for the eastern North Pacific is about 16.

c. the mature hurricane stage

As the tropical storm spins up to a sustained surface wind of at least 74 mph, it becomes a hurricane. The clear or mostly clear eye forms in the center of lowest pressure and the storm grows in strength and size as long as it stays over water at least 79 degrees F. with no shearing affect aloft from another weather system, which would cut off vertical sustenance and therefore diminish or kill the storm.

The envelope of hurricane force wind expands outward from the eye-wall as our hurricane grows, and the area of tropical storm force winds outside the band of hurricane winds, also expands. Under the storm, the waves on the sea will grow to fifteen high and higher. In hurricanes with sustained winds of 140 mph or greater, the waves may be 25 to 40 feet high, and even higher. The waves are caused by the powerful winds and the rapid drop in pressure towards the eye, which in effect lifts some of the water into a dome, especially as the eye approaches the much shallower water near the shore.

The hurricane is a nearly-circular vortex, becoming more symmetrical as it becomes more intense. In the region of hurricane-force winds, the winds are termed CYCLOSTROPHIC, which is a balance between the pressure-gradient force which causes the wind, and the centrifugal force of the curved flow. The Coriolis force is relatively very weak, being greatly overpowered by the centrifugal force in the region of hurricane-force winds. This is especially true in the tropics, where the Coriolis force is weak anyway.

Wind blows from high to low pressure. The pressure difference over a specified distance is the pressure gradient. The west-to-east rotation of the earth creates the Coriolis force which affects moving air parcels by turning them to the right in the Northern Hemisphere and to the left in the Southern Hemisphere. Near the surface (i.e., in the planetary boundary layer), friction prevents a complete 90° turn, but the Coriolis effect is closest to 90 degrees over the oceans, where the frictional component of the wind is less than it is over land.

Most hurricanes have a diameter of some 250 to 500 miles...400 to 800 km. The vertical cyclonic circulation typically extends to near 50,000 feet ...15 km. Compare the size of a typical hurricane to the size of a typical well-developed winter low pressure system (an "extratropical low"). The extratropical low pressure system typically has a diameter of 1000 miles...1600 kilometers...or more. Thus, a tropical cyclone is smaller yet more intense than an extratropical cyclone. In a hurricane, the system is more compact while the winds spin faster and faster towards the center. The hurricane is quasi-symmetrical to symmetrical in appearance, whereas the extratropical low pressure system is not. The hurricane does not have its own frontal system whereas extratropical lows typically form on fronts.

The hurricane is a warm-core system. The extratropical low lifts warm air over cold air, while cold air behind a cold front advances to the storm's rear. Moreover, above a hurricane, at about 200 millibars...about 39,000 feet...we find a high pressure system, which is caused by the rising warm air. The high itself is warm. In an extratropical low pressure system, the system tilts with height towards the cold air. In the Northern Hemisphere, the 850 mb low or trough is about 100 miles to the northwest of the surface low, and the 700 mb low center or trough is about another 100 miles to the northwest of the 850 mb system. The 500 mb system is also displaced to the cold air (to the northwest or to whatever direction the cold air happens to be in), but by 300 and 200 mb, the upper system then becomes vertically stacked since the thermal advections are weaker at those elevations. In the extratropical low, as the cold front catches up with the warm front to occlude the system, the low weakens and subsequently dies, since the main driving force for the system, the thermal advections, end as the air in the system all mixes up. When the low is occluded, the upper level low or trough is directly over the surface system. The hurricane's demise occurs as cold air entrains into the storm and friction over land diminishes it. Moreover, as soon as the hurricane is removed form its chief source of energy, warm, moist air from over warm seas-water, it decreases in intensity.

The hurricane is driven chiefly by convection. Its some-50,000-foot tops are much higher than the 20,000- to 25,000-foot tops of most extratropical lows...whose precipitation is essentially stratiform...nonconvective...although imbedded convection can occur in winter storms, and convection occurs along some cold fronts, even in winter.

When an extratropical low pressure system has a central sea-level pressure below 29.00", it is typically a major storm. A 29.00" sea-level pressure in a hurricane may be only a category 1 or 2 storm. When pressures fall below 28.00", we have a truly great hurricane.

In the hurricane, the lower-level winds spiral inward, accelerating toward lower pressure and reaching maximum speeds around a narrow ring surrounding the pressure center, the eye. (See figures 49 and 50 on hurricane-model circulation.) The air sinks in the eye, warming adiabatically, leading to clear or mostly clear skies there. An anticyclonic outflow aloft out of the hurricane transports some air away from the storm.

The circulation in the vortex generates the eye-wall clouds and a family of spiral rain bands.

The air is forced upward at the narrow ring of maximum winds, and as it spirals outward in a clockwise manner aloft, it carries a canopy of cloudiness which is the hurricane outflow cloud shield.

Inflowing water vapor condenses, warming the interior of the hurricane and lowering its pressure. Strong winds develop because the pressure gradient is strengthening. In the formative phase of the wind-field development, the growth of the storm is slow, partly because the Coriolis force in the tropics is weak and the pressure adjusts to the wind field at first. Later, as the hurricane spins up, the wind field is driven by the pressure differences.

There is a vertical exchange of energy, moisture and momentum (which is related to the wind) in the lower two-thirds of the troposphere. The lifting of evaporated water out of the planetary boundary layer is crucial to hurricane-genesis. Most of the hurricane's energy appears to come from the release of the latent heat of condensation and fusion and from fluxes of sensible heat from the ocean surface.

Can man destroy a hurricane? Hurricane diminution was tried. Silver iodide and other substances, which act as condensation nuclei about which clouds and subsequent precipitation form, was dropped into the eye-region of some hurricanes. The concept was to generate another eye-wall at a farther-out radius from the natural eye-wall, which would result in a decreased pressure-gradient. However, strong hurricanes on their own sometimes go through cycles of multiple, concentric eye-wall formation and replacement. Thus, this experiment ended. Besides, if the condensation heat energy released by one typical hurricane in one day can supply the energy requirements for the entire United States for a half-year, then just how great is man's power to influence a hurricane?

Just how fast can a major hurricane develop? In 1988, Hurricane Gilbert, which grew into a category 5 hurricane, was passing over very warm water in the Caribbean after it left Jamaica. Its central pressure fell from 28.35" (960 mb) to 26.22" (888 mb) in only 24 hours. In the eye-wall of such a fierce hurricane, the sea-level pressure can drop by one inch...about 30 millibars... in a distance of only one mile, indicating a relatively intense pressure gradient force.

In sustaining itself, a hurricane must be able to concentrate heat in the vertical. Thus, winds at all levels within the storm need to be from essentially the same direction. Thus, to the west of the eye, the wind at all levels within the storm would be from the north, in the Northern Hemisphere, and to the north of the eye, the winds would be from the east at all levels. If these winds are sheared aloft by interaction of the hurricane with another weather system, then the storm will weaken and may fall apart.

When the wind-shear enemy of the hurricane is not present, and the storm is over water of at lest 79°F...26°C, then the air is warmed by contact with the water, which gives the air more warmth to feed the storm. That is to say, the air gains measurable heat known as "sensible heat", and is moistened by evaporation from it, i.e., the gaining of latent heat will subsequently be released through the condensation process as the air rises and cools to form clouds and precipitation.

The rising warm air spirals inward towards the center of the storm. The closer these air parcels get to the center, the faster they flow. There is partial conservation of angular momentum, which has been analogized to the effect that occurs when a figure skater spins faster and faster as she or he tucks her/his arms in.

In the eye-wall, where the greatest fury of the storm is occurring, the air that is spiralling in and rising is cooling, forming more clouds and rain. The latent heat of condensation is released in this process, which cause the air to rise even more. This additional lift results in even more condensation. Thus, we find a rapidly rising column of air, which produces the low pressure center.

The reason for the anticyclonic outflow aloft is that if the air were not removed, the pressure at the center of the hurricane would rise, causing the storm to die. Some of the air, however, moves inward to sink within the eye itself.

Thus, at the top of the eye-wall, air is being propelled outward, and is replaced by rising air within the eye-wall. **The intensity of the anticyclonic outflow is therefore proportional to the intensity of the hurricane.**

How efficient is a hurricane? How much of the energy available to the hurricane does it convert into wind, for example? Some research suggests that only a small percentage of energy is converted into wind. Frankly, we just do not know what we would like to know about energy availability and transformations related to a hurricane, so this is a good research project.

The figure on the following page shows Hurricane Elena, which in 1985 was in the eastern Gulf of Mexico, heading towards the Florida panhandle, when she stopped and then headed southeastward towards the Tampa area, and later stopped and then headed north-northwestward back towards the Florida panhandle, finally coming ashore.

As an aside note of interest: on September 23rd, 1885, a hurricane combined with an early season cold wave to produce 12 inches of snow at Stowe, Vermont.

Figure 53. Hurricane Elena of 1985 in the eastern Gulf of Mexico off Florida. (source: NASA; this picture was taken by astronauts aboard the Space Shuttle Discovery)

d. the dissipating stage

Hurricanes dissipate for any of the following reasons:

●Hurricanes dissipate when they move over land and stay over land. , The friction caused by the land's interaction with the hurricane's winds diminishes the winds' fury. Moreover, the storm is removed from its source of energy, the warm moist air over the warm ocean water.

●Hurricanes decrease in intensity when they pass over water that is cooler than 79°F...26°C. When a hurricane stays over cool water long enough, it loses tropical characteristics and is no longer a tropical cyclone.

●The upper levels of a hurricane can be sheared away by interaction with another strong weather system. The rising spiralling-in air and the anticyclonic outflow aloft are disrupted, killing the hurricane. When a minimal hurricane or a tropical storm moves to the right of a powerful hurricane but is so close that the anticyclonic outflow of the bigger storm lashes across it, the weaker storm is killed. This happened in 1989 by powerful Hurricane Hugo shearing Tropical Storm Iris to his southwest.

●A minimal hurricane or a tropical storm can be absorbed by a powerful one if it gets too close to it. Another tropical storm named Iris was absorbed by a large hurricane named Humberto in 1995.

●As a powerful hurricane, a category 3 or higher, passes over the open ocean, it will churn up the water and can create a temporary upwelling of colder water. This colder water will remain in the area over which the storm passed, for several days. A successive tropical cyclone passing over the same ocean area which has this upwelled water, will be affected by it if the water temperature is below 79 degrees Fahrenheit by diminishing. This scenario occurred in 1995 after powerful Hurricane Luis passed between the United States and Bermuda, causing a cool pool of water in its wake. Several days later, Hurricane Marilyn passed over this cool pool and stopped strengthening, then diminished in intensity.

As the hurricane dies, the eye fills with clouds and the circulation around the storm slackens. In higher latitudes, the tropical cyclone is likely to interact with fronts and extratropical lows, merging into an extratropical low, or having its remnants picked up by a moving frontal system.

A hurricane that has been dissipating yet still maintains some circulation, can reintensify if it moves back over warm waters and is not being sheared.

e. sea-surface temperatures and hurricanes.

As has already been discussed, a tropical cyclone requires a sea-surface temperature of at least 79°F, 26°C, for genesis and intensification. Warmer water means warmer air above it which means higher dewpoints, consequently giving the hurricane more energy to be released in the heat of condensation during cloud and precipitation development.

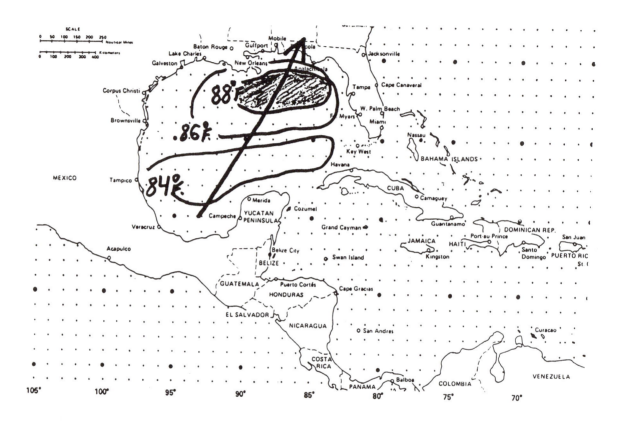

Figure 54. Water surface temperatures in the Gulf of Mexico during Hurricane Opal of 1995, and Opal's path. Opal intensified rapidly as she passed over the pool of temperatures in the mid-to-upper 80s F. Had she not been moving at a forward speed of 20 mph and faster, she would likely have had another day or two to continue intensifying over the very warm water, and may have struck the Gulf Coast as a category 4 or 5 hurricane, similar to Superhurricane Camille of 1969.

Typhoons of the western North Pacific tend to be larger and, on the average, more powerful than their hurricane cousins of the North Atlantic Basin because they have larger region of very warm ocean surface temperatures over which to traverse. Therefore, many typhoons have more time over very warm water to keep intensifying.

PAGE 90

Powerful hurricanes can churn up the ocean surface, mixing the water and bringing up cooler water from below, which can persist for several days to about a couple of weeks. The much lower pressure in and immediately around the eye lifts the water up in a dome of up to a few feet underneath the eye area. This also helps to pull up some cooler water from below to replace some water displaced by the wind and low pressure.

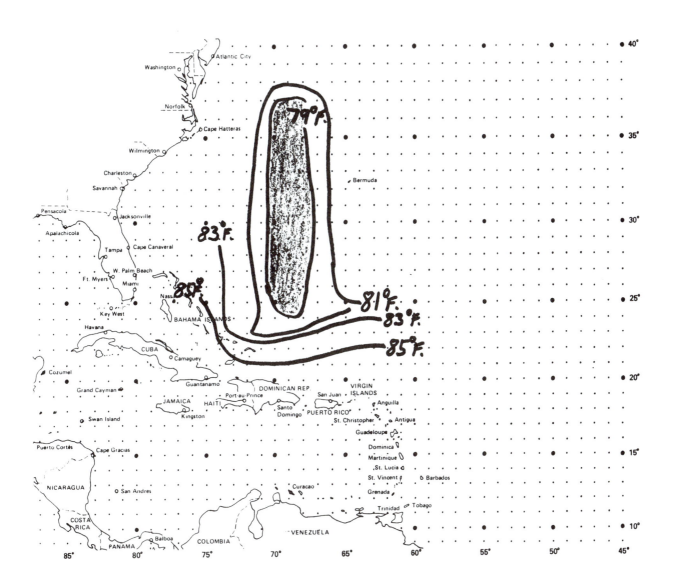

Figure 55. Unusually cool waters were in the region from 70W to 68W and 24N to 37N on September 17th, 1995. Sea-surface temperatures were some 5 to 6 degrees F. lower than they were before Hurricanes Felix and Luis passed over the area. These lower temperatures helped to kill Hurricane Marilyn, which passed over this cool pool, following close to Luis' path.

6. THE NAMING OF HURRICANES

Figure 56. Hurricane names are agreed to by a committee under the World Meteorological Organization (WMO), an agency of the United Nations. The WMO Regional Association IV (North America) Hurricane Operational Plan sets the names. If, in the North Atlantic Basin, a year's 21 names are exhausted, then the letters of the Greek alphabet are used in order. Thus, for example, if this year's #21 named Atlantic Basin storm were Wendy, and three more tropical cyclones developed in the year, they would be named, respectively, Alpha, Beta and Gamma. The rule as written actually applies to the eastern North Pacific Basin but is inferred for the North Atlantic.

The decision to give hurricanes names so that they could be catalogued, remembered and referenced by name may have been inspired by an old book entitled, "STORM", by George R. Stewart, published in 1941, which was a fiction novel about a monster low pressure system that crosses the Pacific and moves across the United States, causing considerable havoc. The author gave the storm the name, "Maria". Recall the words to the song, "They call the wind Maria".

During and after World War II, the radio-code phonetic alphabet was in place, with A for Able, B for Baker, C for Charlie, etc. Later, a new phonetic alphabet replaced this one, but in the early 1950s, with the original phonetic alphabet in place, the United States Weather Bureau began assigning these names sequentially to tropical storms and hurricanes. A tropical depression or wave was not given a name. The system had to spin up to tropical storm force, 39 mph sustained winds, before it was assigned a name.

The first officially named storms in the North Atlantic Basin were in 1950, from Hurricane Able through Hurricane Love. (One unnamed storm was discovered after the fact to have spent its life in the eastern Atlantic.) In 1951, there were ten tropical cyclones, from Hurricane Able to Hurricane Jig, and in 1952 there was an unusual tropical storm in early February which went unnamed until later, after the fact, it was termed a tropical storm after it lashed south Florida, Cape Cod and Maine, and then moved into New Brunswick Province, Canada. By the end of the 1952 hurricane season, it was obvious that there would be a problem of referencing if a major hurricane, say an Able, struck the east coast one year, followed by another major hurricane named Able a year or two later. Thus, different sets of names needed to be used, with rotation rates of several years between sets. Then, when a major hurricane strikes a populous region, that name could be retired for at least a few generations.

Thus, in 1953 the North Atlantic Basin tropical cyclones had people names for the first time. This turned out to be a timely idea, since 1954, 1955 and 1956 had a series of major hurricanes causing widespread damage and flooding along the east coast.

The first such-named storm was Tropical Storm Alice in 1953. All tropical storms and hurricanes were at that time given female names, almost all of which were two-syllable names. This practice was changed in 1979 when male names were added, although male and female names were started in the eastern Pacific the prior year. The number of syllables in a name is no longer a consideration factor.

The first male tropical cyclone in the North Atlantic Basin, in July 1979, was Hurricane Bob. Two of the first male hurricanes, David and Frederic in 1979, picked as their first target the Virgin Islands.

Names are now chosen to reflect the three main languages of North America...English, Spanish and French.

A committee of the World Meteorological Organization, a small unit under the United Nations, agrees to the list of names.

In the North Atlantic Basin, 21 names are assigned for each year. The letters q, u, x, y and z are not used, although this is a leftover from when the names were only in English. Now, with two other languages, at least some of these letters could be later added in. If, as in the 1995 hurricane season, we have so many hurricanes that the list is almost depleted or actually does get used up, the WMO directive is to then use the letters of the Greek alphabet, in sequence, to name the storms. Thus, a Wendy would be followed by Tropical Storm or Hurricane Alpha, then Beta, Gamma, Delta, Epsilon, etc. If one of the Greek-named hurricanes were a major storm that struck land and needed to have its name retired, then, theoretically, that name could not be used again for a few generations, if we had another season within a few generations that had more than 21 named systems. As stated before, the Greek-letter names are for the eastern North Pacific which typically has more tropical cyclones than does the North Atlantic, but the rule is inferred for the North Atlantic Basin.

These rules are man-made, and as such can always be changed. The above is the policy as of this writing.   PAGE 93

A different set of names exists for the eastern North Pacific, and yet another for the central North Pacific for hurricanes forming in the Hawaiian jurisdiction. This does not preclude an eastern Pacific hurricane from moving into the Hawaiian area.

In the western Pacific, a separate set is also used for the typhoons, and a specific set is also used for Indian Ocean tropical cyclones.

Winter arctic hurricanes are not tropical systems and so far are not named.

One somewhat aggravating oversight that may be corrected is the unfortunate practice of renaming a storm when it moves from one basin to another. For example, when a hurricane crosses Central America from the Atlantic into the Pacific, it immediately takes on a new name from the list for the basin it moved into. This ruins continuity for identification purposes for following the history of the same storm. In the 1980s one Atlantic tropical storm had a gender change when it emerged into the Pacific.

Occasionally, an eastern Pacific hurricane crosses the International Dateline and is no longer a hurricane, but a typhoon, and acquires a name change.

Perhaps the issue may be discussed at the World Meteorological Organization. The only damage done is to referencing the entire history of the same storm with its original identifying name.

In 1993, Tropical Storm Bret, skirting the north coast of South America, moved into the Pacific to become Hurricane Greg. In 1994, Hurricane Kristy of the eastern Pacific diminished in intensity but then regenerated as Typhoon Melissa in the western Pacific.

In September 1978, Atlantic Hurricane Greta crossed Belize, Guatemala and part of south Mexico to become Pacific Hurricane Olivia. In September 1974, Hurricane Fifi skirted Honduras, crossed Belize and Guatemala and then went through part of southern Mexico into the Pacific Ocean to become Pacific Hurricane Orlene.

In September 1971, Hurricane Irene crossed Nicaragua to become a powerful eastern Pacific hurricane named Olivia.

There are other examples of storms crossing into another "jurisdiction"; these name-changes are offered to illustrate that such occurs from time to time.

An unusual far-low-latitude tropical cyclone was an unnamed hurricane that occurred in late September 1969 forming off the east coast of Costa Rica and north coast of Panama. Note that in the western part of Panama, you can travel from west to east and go from the Atlantic to the Pacific Ocean. This hurricane apparently died over Panama at about 8 degrees North latitude.

In 1902, 1923 and 1949, tropical cyclones formed in the eastern Pacific and crossed into the Atlantic Basin into the Gulf of Mexico. Also, the remnants of many Pacific hurricanes have crossed from Mexico into the United States central plains and even to the east coast, producing flash flooding or heavy rains.

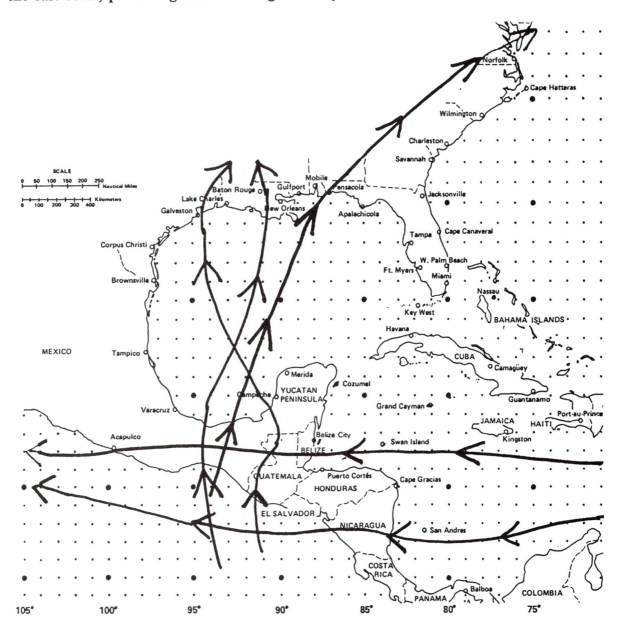

Figure 57. Examples of actual tracks of tropical cyclones that originated in the North Atlantic Basin or the Eastern North Pacific Basin and crossed over into the other basin to be tropical cyclones there.

7. HURRICANES AS DEPICTED ON WEATHER RADAR

Doppler weather radars depict the precipitation as well as the radial component of the wind. The first (pre-Doppler) weather radars were installed along the east and Gulf coasts of the U.S. because of the hurricane threat. Recall that the first weather satellite, TIROS I, did not exist until 1960. Thus, we did not want hurricanes to sneak up on any coastal area.

The weather surveillance radars developed by 1957 were called just that -WSR-57s. A newer generation of radars began in 1974 with the WSR-74s. Then came the WSR-88Ds, the Doppler weather radars.

Most radars operate on a range of 125 nautical miles, with a longer range going to some 250 nautical miles.

It might be useful here to quickly look again at figure 39 on page 64, showing a radar composite average of the typical hurricane.

The radar sends out a beam of electromagnetic energy which, if sent out at the appropriate wavelength...from 5 to 10 centimeters...will reflect off precipitation targets, with some of the reflected energy being received by the radar antenna and electronically processed for depiction on a monitor. The radar antenna rotates as it sends out a beam of energy, but most of the time it is in the listening phase, for detecting reflected energy from precipitation. We could have one radar transmitting a beam continually, but that would require another system to detect any reflected energy, and two systems are not cost-effective.

The more intense the rainfall, the stronger will be the energy return. Thus, the radar ECHOES can be depicted in greater shades of white for increasingly heavier precipitation, or can be colorized, with, for example, green for the lightest rain, yellow for moderate, orange for heavy, red for very heavy and purple for intense. This scheme is exceptionally useful for tracking not only the hurricane precipitation, but the storm itself, since, knowing the structure of a hurricane, the radar shows the external hurricane squall-line, outer convective bands, rain shield, eye-wall and the eye when these features pass within radar range. The movement of the system can be measured by tracking the eye on radar, although new formations and dissipations of the convective line segments that comprise the eye-wall exhibit a wobbly movement of the eye. Moreover, sometimes a new concentric outer eye-wall forms in intense hurricanes and moves inward to replace the original eye-wall. Despite all of this, the AVERAGE movement of the eye...of the hurricane... is trackable by radar.

As far back as 1961, a study found that the position of the hurricane's eye wobbled as much as three miles within five minutes from the average or smoothed track.

A wobbling-appearance of the eye track is can also be caused by other factors, including intensity changes of the hurricane itself (recall that the eye generally shrinks as the storm intensifies), the large-scale flow-pattern exerts an influence on the storm's movement, there are some asymmetrical aspects to the storm, especially in minimal hurricanes, there are effects of friction, there is an effect because of any vertical tilting of the system, and the storm's intensity itself may affect its path.

Sometimes the hurricane hunter aircraft may locate the center adjacent to the most convectively active part of the eye-wall, rather than exactly in the middle of the eye, especially in minimal, developing hurricanes.   Thus, the geometric center of the hurricane is not always pinpointed in the middle of its changing eye.

Figure 58. Construction of the radar dome, called radome, and pedestal of a Doppler radar system. The rotating and tiltable antenna is located within the approximately 10-meter wide radome.

Following are some radar displays of different hurricanes in various stages of intensity and various locations in relation to the respective radar sites. Note how the rainbands, rain shield, eye-wall and eye appear on radar.

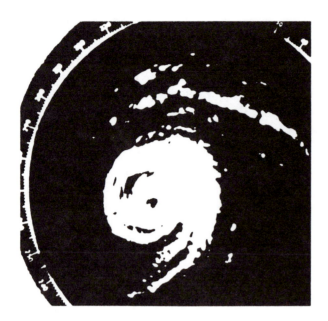

Figure 59. Two radar displays of hurricanes, showing precipitation echoes. The radar image at left is from a radar on the 250 nautical mile long range. The eye is southwest of the radar site, which is in the center of the scope, and the spiral bands are evidenced by their precipitation to the south of the storm center. To the north and northeast of the main part of the storm is an outer-hurricane squall-line and outer convective bands. The radar image at the right is from a radar on the short range, or 125 nmi. range. Each concentric circle on the display is 25 nautical miles apart from another circle. Here, the eye is just south-southwest of the radar site. Its rain-free area shows the eye to be just over 40 nmi. in diameter. (source: NWS)

Figure 60. An accumulated rainfall display from the WSR88-D radar. The Doppler radar computer system processes the data it measures, also utilizing algorithms (problem-solving techniques) to give displays such as this one. The display is actually in color, with different colors corresponding to different radar-derived rainfall totals over a period of time. Other Doppler displays include the radial velocity of the wind at different levels, and algorithm-based warnings of radar signatures of hail and tornadoes. Hail is rare in a hurricane, and when it does occur it is small and does not last long. (source: NOAA)

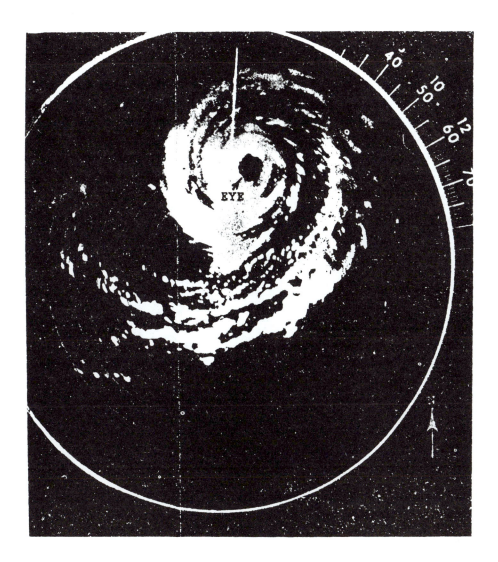

Figure 61. Hurricane Donna, which raked the east coast from Florida to New England, as she appeared on the Key West, Florida weather radar, on the short range, on September 10, 1960. The eye at this time was to the north-northeast of Key West and shows up nicely as a quasi-circular echo-free center of the hurricane. The rain shield surrounds the eye-wall and the spiral bands are evident. Donna began just off the west African coast on August 29th, slashed across Florida and came up the east coast, crossing coastal North Carolina and then slamming across Long Island and into New England on September 12th. She moved through southeastern Canada and died over the cold waters of the North Atlantic. Hurricane Donna was a memorable storm for many people who lived there at the time, since it affected the entire east cost of the United States from Florida to Maine. Several weeks earlier, in July, Tropical Storm Brenda formed rapidly in the eastern Gulf of Mexico and took a path that was just to the left of Donna's, also affecting the entire east coast. (source: NOAA)

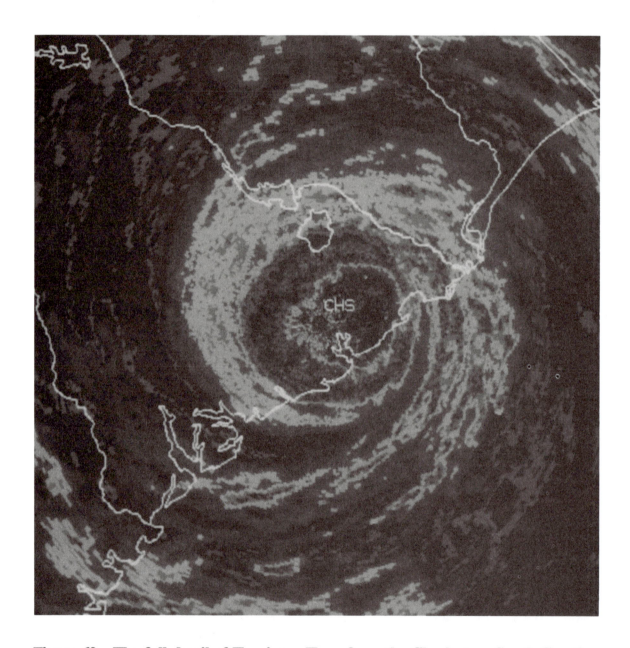

Figure 62. The full detail of Hurricane Hugo from the Charleston, South Carolina weather radar as Hugo's eye makes landfall just north of Charleston in Sept. 1989. (source: NOAA - Hurricane Research Division)

8. HURRICANES AS DEPICTED ON WEATHER SATELLITE IMAGERY

There are two types of meteorological satellites: geosynchronous and polar-orbiting. The geosynchronous satellites are placed in an orbit 22,300 miles from earth, over the equator, so that they can move from west to east, the same as the earth, at the same rotational speed of the earth at the equator, about 1000 mph. Since the circumference of the earth is about 25,000 miles, the earth, rotating at a little over 1000 mph at the equator, makes its complete rotation in 24 hours, with the geosynchronous satellites moving at the same speed, and therefore staying over the same location.

The current family of geosynchronous satellites is called GOES, which stands for "Geostationary Operational Environmental Satellite". Five GOES systems circle the globe, all over the equator. One is off the east coast of the Americas and one is off the west coast of the Americas. The others are at about the longitude of Japan (south of Japan), over the Indian Ocean and over Africa. Thus, the world is covered.

The other family of meteorological satellites is the polar orbiter series. These satellites are at a much lower altitude, about 1000 miles out, and are placed in an orbit that roughly goes from pole to pole, taking images in a swath averaging some 1500 miles across.

The main weather satellite images are visible, infrared, enhanced infrared and water vapor imagery. Images are returned to ground stations on earth, processed and enhanced to depict the weather features.

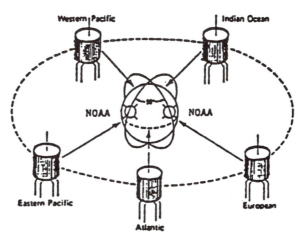

Figure 63. A schematic depicting the geosynchronous GOES weather satellites in orbits 22,300 miles out, and the polar orbiter weather satellites, currently known as NOAA satellites, in quasi-pole-to-pole orbits several hundred miles out. The GOES satellites stay over the same locations over the equator, sending images of the same part of the globe from North to South polar regions. In very high latitudes, cloud tops are displaced farther poleward by GOES satellites, which is why the polar orbiters are more useful in polar regions.

a. visible weather satellite imagery

Figure 64. A visible weather satellite picture of a well-developed hurricane. The features of the hurricane are well-defined: spiral feeder bands, rain shield, eye-wall and the eye. Visible images are available, obviously, only during the daylight. Infrared images are available during both daylight and nighttime. (source: NOAA)

Figure 65. A hurricane as depicted by visible imagery from a polar-orbiting weather satellite. Notice the large clear eye quite evident in the picture. (source: NOAA, National Climatic Data Center)

Figure 66. With the detection by weather satellite (left photo) and weather radar (right photo), hurricanes can not strike coastal areas with a surprise hit. (source: NOAA)

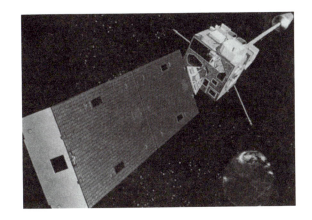

Figure 67. A look at Hurricane Andrew of 1992 in a visible image from a geosynchronous weather satellite. Note the spiralling-in counterclockwise circulation of the clouds, the solid cloudmass of the rainshield and the clear circular eye of the hurricane. Andrew's eye remained intact as the hurricane crossed the flat low-elevation terrain of the Florida Everglades. (source: NOAA, Tropical Prediction Center, National Hurricane Center)

b. enhanced infrared weather satellite imagery

At night, visible pictures are not possible; therefore, infrared technology is used. Infrared images are also taken during the daytime.

Infrared radiation is a form of heat. The earth and clouds emit infrared radiation. Therefore, sensors have been developed for the weather satellites to detect the amount of radiation being emitted by the cloud tops and, if no clouds are present, by the targets below (the ground, ocean surface or snow- or ice-covered surfaces).

On an infrared black-and-white image, colder objects appear white and warmer objects appear black. Thus, if we were comparing a weather satellite picture in the visible with an image in the infrared, with both showing part of the earth and its clouds and also past the curve of the earth to show outer space, then cold outer space would appear black in the visible picture and white in the infrared image.

In meteorology, we have developed what are called "enhancement curves" which cause the infrared image to depict temperature ranges in shades of gray, white and black. Thus, we can start the enhancement at some desired temperature that would give some idea of the height of the cloud tops, and use a medium gray for say -32°C to -41°C, then a light gray for -42 to -52 degrees, etc., followed by a dark gray, then black , then white. We can set black to represent cloud tops colder than -62°C, which would mean very impressive thunderstorms if these clouds are the tops of thunderstorms. If they are, then the white, set at -80°C or colder, would represent very cold tops, i.e., very high-topped thunderstorms, likely 50,000 to 60,000 feet high and even higher (in mid-latitudes), and would be associated with the heaviest rainfall, maybe flash-flood producing, and/or the most severe weather, since these "overshooting tops", which are overshooting the rest of the thunderstorm or thunderstorm complex, represent the area(s) likely having the strongest convective updrafts.

We can also colorize these different enhancement levels, making them easy to interpret plus visually more stunning, as we observe them on computer monitors or in a color image picture.

Infrared imagery has limitations. Ground targets such as fog and snow-cover do not show up well. Thus, professional and amateur meteorologists look at both visible and infrared images during the daytime, and infrared images at night, to identify features. The infrared imagery most commonly used is enhanced infrared imagery. Moreover, another type of infrared depiction called the "water vapor imagery" is used to detect moisture in the troposphere, whether in cloud form or not, between approximately 10,000 and 30,000 feet up, which is essentially between about 700 and 300 mb. Water vapor imagery will be discussed later.

Figure 68. Compare the visible picture of Hurricane Frederic of 1979 (top) with an enhanced infrared image of the same storm (bottom) (the infrared image is enlarged somewhat to show the detail). Gray areas on the outer part of Frederic are clouds at cirrus-level, and the black area of the hurricane is the rain shield, within which a large white area represents the coldest cloud tops and most intense convective rainfall. (source: NOAA)

Thus, the most intense rainfall of the storm, which tends to correlate with the fiercest winds in the storm, can be followed in the enhanced infrared weather satellite imagery. Video-loops easily identify development, movement and diminution of the hurricane.

PAGE 106

c. hurricanes on water vapor imagery

Figure 69. A water vapor image from a GOES weather satellite. The milky white areas are moisture in the air, not in cloud form, and the bright white areas are moisture which has condensed into clouds, most of the data being detected between approximately 10,000 and 30,000 feet up, thus the water vapor image depicts MID- AND UPPER-LEVEL MOISTURE, WHETHER IN CLOUD FORM OR NOT. ("Mid- and upper-level" refers to the middle and upper portions of the troposphere, respectively.) Note the clouds and moisture in the intertropical convergence zone just north of the equator. There is a developing tropical cyclone off the west coast of Mexico. (source: NOAA)

Here is the physical basis for water vapor satellite images. The earth receives radiation from the sun in many frequencies, short-wave and long-wave, converting that radiation to energy forms which include heat, which is a form of long-wave radiation. The earth, and clouds, emit this heat, which is the infrared radiation sensed by the weather satellites.

(continued)

At the 6.7 micrometer wavelength, which is a part of the infrared band, water vapor in the air has the property of absorbing this infrared radiation. It then reemits it. Thus, a sensor on a satellite can be designed to measure the flux of radiation from targets emitting radiation at 6.7 micrometers. The amount of radiation received is proportional to the temperature of the emittor., which is the basis for enhancement of infrared images. Moreover, the more moisture in the depth of atmosphere being sensed, the brighter the area will appear on the water vapor image.

Therefore, moisture that is not or not yet condensed into cloud form appears a fuzzy or a milky light white, whereas clouds appear bright white. Areas that are relatively dry and/or are drying due to subsiding air, show up dark.

Recall that water vapor imagery sensing works essentially for the 10,000- to 30,000-foot range depth of atmosphere, essentially sensing moisture between about 700 and 300 millibars (hectoPascals).

Looking at a water vapor image is analogous to looking at a fog from the top down. The more of it there is, and/or the greater its vertical extent, the thicker it will appear.

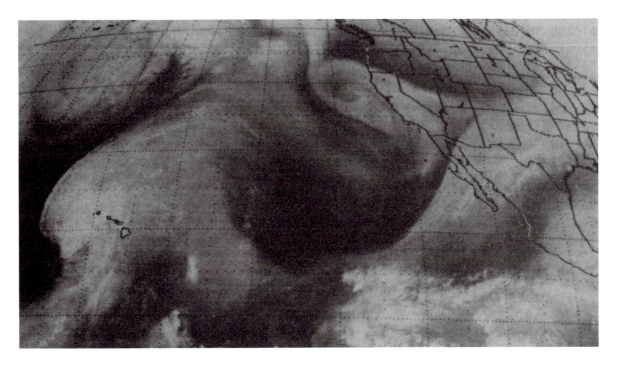

Figures 70, top, and 71, bottom. Visible satellite picture, top, and water vapor image, bottom, of Hurricane Iwa approaching the Hawaiian Islands on November 23rd, 1982. (source: NOAA)

The infrared image shows the greater extent of the mid- and upper-level moisture associated with Iwa. The water vapor image also helps to identify the location of the upper-level anticyclonic cirrroform outflow aloft, located to the north and northeast of the storm center.

Figure 72. A Western Hemispheric full-disk visible picture view from a GOES weather satellite. The relative size and scope of a huge superhurricane, Allen (19Z Aug. 7th, 1980), in the Gulf of Mexico, and a routine hurricane, Isis, off the west coast of Mexico. (source: NOAA)

d. estimating hurricane intensity from satellite imagery

Hurricanes have specific recognizable signatures in the satellite imagery. This concept is utilized in estimating the strength of a tropical cyclone by its appearance on both visible and enhanced infrared imagery.

V. J. Dvorak wrote a landmark technical paper in 1984 entitled, "Tropical Cyclone Intensity Analysis Using Satellite Data". This technique is quite helpful in determining the strength of a tropical cyclone far out in the eastern Atlantic if no hurricane reconnaissance aircraft are assigned to gather data on the system. Even when the hurricane hunters are flying into the storm, the satellite intensity estimates provide additional confirmation about the storm. Moreover, the hurricane hunters are not continually in the storm, whereas the continuous stream of weather satellite data allows us to keep current on the storm's estimated intensity and evolution.

The best and most complete data set is taken by the reconnaissance aircraft hurricane hunters. The winds at flight level of 2000 to 1500 feet are extrapolated to the somewhat lower speed estimate for the surface winds. The barometric pressure in the eye, and the eye's diameter and characteristics are observed. Wave heights under the eye are estimated. The hurricane hunters fly out of the eye-wall into the relatively calm eye at an angle, because the wind-shear is extreme in passing from hurricane-intensity sustained winds to a sudden near calm, and vice versa. The aircraft does lower to the 1500- to 2000-foot flight level to obtain the wind speed measurements so that the maximum winds can be reported. All of this is not possible through a satellite measurement; however, the Dvorak technique does relate the appearance of the storm on weather satellite imagery with likely wind speeds.

Dvorak rates the storms on a "T" scale, the T standing for "Tropical Cyclone". As shown by the graphic on the following page, T2.5 is the appearance of a minimal tropical storm, T3.5 is the threshold value of a strong tropical storm, T4.5 is a minimal hurricane, T5.5 is a strong hurricane and T6.5 or higher is a superhurricane.

Figure 73. DVORAK TROPICAL CYCLONE INTENSITY ESTIMATION FROM WEATHER SATELLITE IMAGERY

Developmental cloud pattern types used in intensity analysis.

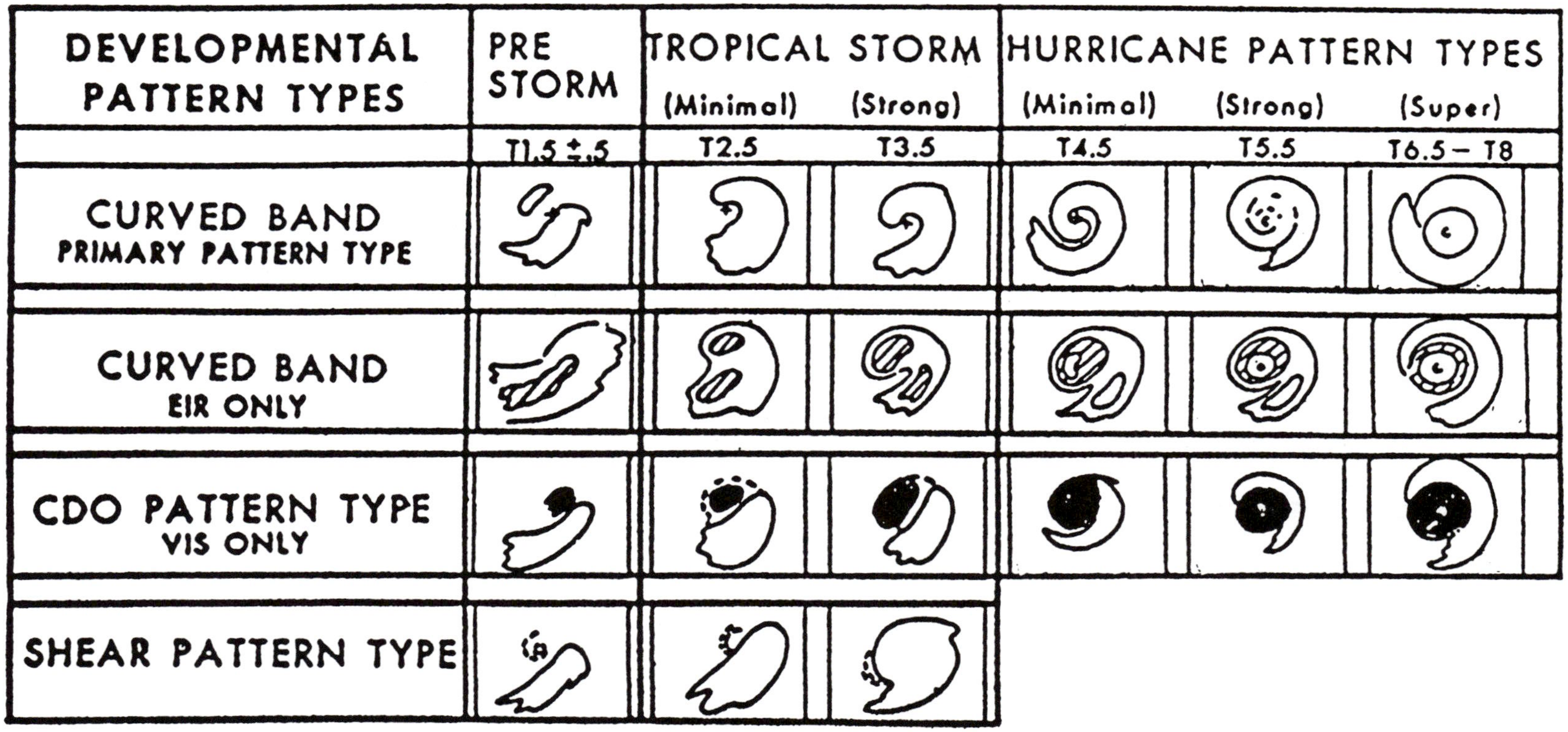

9. HURRICANE MOVEMENTS AND TRACKS

The track of a tropical cyclone is plotted as the path of the location of the center of the eye, which should be the location of the lowest sea-level atmospheric pressure. However, the eye-wall is comprised on lines of convection, which individually grow, mature and die, continually being replaced by new eye-wall segments. In powerful hurricanes, a concentric outer eye sometimes develops and moves inward, replacing the inner eye. This process is accompanied by intensity fluctuations in the storm.

Thus, the path of the storm is typically not a smooth line or curve, but a wobbly path which, when averaged, is a smooth line or curve.

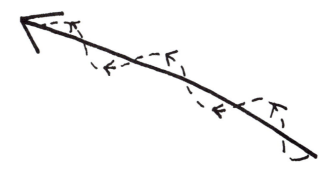

Figure 74. A segment of the path of a hurricane. The solid line shows the average track and the dashed line depicts the actual movement of the center of the eye. The hurricane's eye oscillates or wobbles along its average path as it moves along.

The evolution of the convective lines of the eye-wall are best observed by weather radar when the hurricane's eye, still over the ocean, is within range of a coastal radar, especially if the eye is no more than about 125 nautical miles from the radar site.

One study as far back as 1961, just some four years after the introduction of coastal network weather radars, found that the average hurricane's eye wobbled as much as three miles in five minutes.

Recall that the eye does not appear until the storm's sustained winds reach approximately hurricane intensity, with one study suggesting just above minimal hurricane strength. While the system is a tropical storm, its path is traced by the location of the minimum pressure, since no eye exists.

The eye's path does not always wobble, but it often exhibits this behavior. Keep in mind that besides the ongoing evolutionary process of the convective lines that comprise the eye-wall, there are other factors affecting the storm's forward motion.

(continued)

As stated earlier in this manuscript, the following are some of the factors causing the hurricane's eye to wobble on its path:

●the large-scale flow pattern exerts an influence on the storm's movement;

●there are asymmetric aspects to most hurricanes;

●there are effects of friction;

●there is an effect because of any vertical tilting of the system; and

●the intensity of the storm itself may affect its path.

Since most hurricanes form in the tropics, they move with an east-to-west component of motion, steered by the trade winds in that region. During North Atlantic hurricane season, the strength of the huge Bermuda-Azores high pressure system over the ocean also helps steer the incipient tropical system around its southern periphery. Farther west, the western extent of this high has a southeasterly wind flow, which helps to turn the tropical system to the northwest. The farther wet the Bermuda-Azores high is situated, and the stronger it is, the farther westward travels the tropical cyclone before it begins its veering to the northwest.

Farther north, the storm becomes increasingly under the influence of the mid-latitude westerlies and continues its veering towards the north, then northeast and out into the cold waters of the North Atlantic to either die, become absorbed into an extratropical low pressure system, becoming for a while a hybrid tropical/subtropical system, or having its remnants continue for a while.

Each tropical cyclone has its own unique path because of the various factors involved in steering the system.

Sometimes, a superhurricane becomes so large and powerful that its movement defies the steering forces on it so that the storm moves essentially through its own energy and momentum. Hurricane Allen of 1980 was such a storm. It was so massive that at one time it covered the entire Gulf of Mexico. Allen's lowest reported sea-level barometer reading was 26.55".

Another superhurricane that defied predicting was Gilbert of 1988. Although numerical forecast computer models had Gilbert projected to turn to the northwest to affect the central Gulf Coast around Louisiana, Gilbert plowed ahead for four consecutive days to the west-northwest at about 14 mph with no deviation in forward direction or speed. Gilbert's lowest pressure was 26.22".

The next year, all the computer forecast models had Hurricane Hugo, after striking the South Carolina coast, turning to the north-northeast to come up to the coast to affect New Jersey, New York City, Long Island and New England. Instead, Hugo tracked from about Charleston, South Carolina to around Charleston, West Virginia before recurving.

Forecasting the precise movement of a hurricane for beyond 24 hours can be a challenge. The problem is exacerbated by the fact that many weather forecasters suffer from "Meteorological AIDS: the Artificial Intelligence Dependency Syndrome". This is when a forecaster looks at forecast outputs from a series of computer forecast models and accepts this as the forecast, not even using his/her own meteorological knowledge to make the prediction. This is especially true when all the models forecast essentially the same prognosis, as in the forecast for Hurricane Hugo, yet they are all wrong!

Our forecast models have become rudimentarally sophisticated to the point at which it would be foolish to ignore their outputs, but it is also wrong to always rely on them as the "gospel truth" because their outputs are not.

Thus, the solution to Meteorological AIDS, if you are a weather forecaster, is to make your own forecast based on your meteorological expertise, and then compare it with the output from the models. Use the model forecasts as GUIDANCE, not as the forecast. Then massage your prognosis with those of the models to make the best possible forecast. Obviously, a knowledge of how the models work is essential, along with having documentation of the biases of each model (for example, does one model tend to recurve the hurricane too soon).

A typical example of a tough hurricane of which to forecast its motion was Hurricane Roxanne of October 1995. Roxanne came out of the western Caribbean, moved across Mexico's Yucatan Peninsula, and emerged over the Bay of Campeche in the southwest Gulf of Mexico. Most models, including statistical models which have input from past hurricanes, forecasted Roxanne to move southwestward across southern Mexico, which would bring her into the eastern Pacific where she would have been forced to assume a new name. Instead, Roxanne made a loop in the Bay of Campeche and began drifting northwestward. Thus, models alone are the wrong answer to hurricane prediction, but they are quite helpful almost all of the time for guidance. The hurricane specialists at the National Hurricane Center/Tropical Prediction Center realize this, and as you read their forecasts, you will notice that they typically take model compromises based on model performance and give their reasoning for projecting the path of a tropical storm or hurricane. They are also honest in giving their reliability on projections, especially for projections beyond about 36 hours. Thus, although we have learned much about tropical cyclones, the passion for more research continues.

Following are examples of tropical storm and hurricane tracks from three representative years, chosen because they show more-or-less typical paths of these storms in the North Atlantic Basin.

Figures 75 and 76. Tracks of North Atlantic Basin tropical storms and hurricanes in two separate years, showing examples of the types of paths these storms can take. (source: National Hurricane Center)

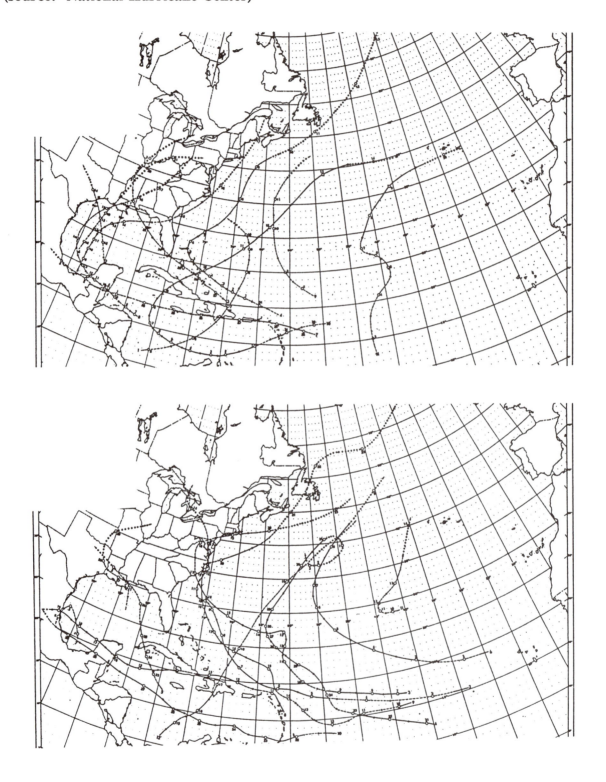

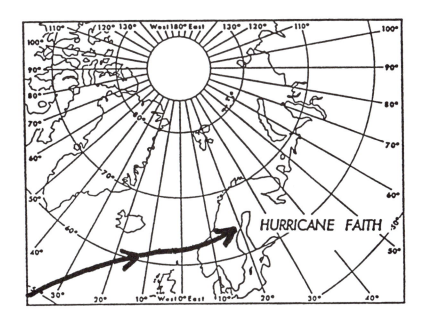

Figure 77. The track of a most unusual hurricane, Hurricane Faith of 1966. Faith formed off the west African coast, crossed the Atlantic to approach the Carolinas, then veered to the northeast, accelerating to a forward speed of over 50 mph when she finally made landfall in Norway on September 6th. Faith continued on into Sweden. By the time she made landfall, Faith was rapidly acquiring extratropical characteristics as cold air entered her circulation. Nevertheless, Hurricane Faith of 1966 is an example of a rare event: a hurricane forming along the west coast of Africa, travelling across the Atlantic to return across the Atlantic, and striking Scandinavia in northern Europe. (source: National Hurricane Center)

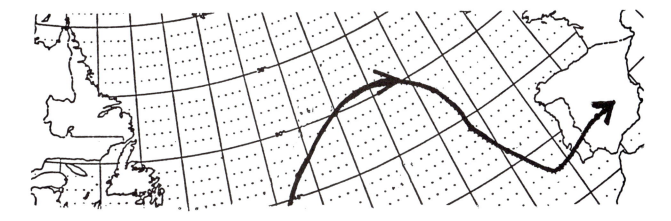

Figure 78. Another unusual hurricane, Hurricane Arlene of August 1987, which moved into Portugal and Spain as a weakened storm. Arlene formed over the Bahama Islands off south Florida, and three times, after heading northeastward, turned to the southeast for a while. After her last southeast turn, Arlene turned to the northeast for the fourth time and moved into Portugal and Spain, causing record rainfall at Rota, Spain. (source: National Hurricane Center)

10. THE FIERCE WINDS OF A HURRICANE

Easterly waves, West African Disturbance Lines and other seedlings may not have sustained winds of any significance, but likely have gusty winds in the their thunderstorms. When a circulation begins to develop, the system becomes a tropical depression. Sustained winds may reach 20 to 35 mph.

When the sustained winds reach the 39 mph threshold, the depression is upgraded to a tropical storm and acquires a name. When these winds reach the 74 mph threshold, the tropical storm is upgraded to a hurricane.

Similarly, as a hurricane diminishes, it goes through the diminishing categorization from hurricane to tropical storm and then to either tropical depression, hybrid storm, or evolving into an extratropical storm. The former hurricane may become absorbed by an extratropical low pressure system or, as in 1995's Tropical Storm Iris case, be absorbed by another, stronger and larger tropical cyclone (Iris was absorbed by Hurricane Humberto). Also, the remnants of a hurricane may move on as an area of showers and thunderstorms until it dies or part or all of it is absorbed into another system.

In the North Atlantic Basin, there were only a few occasions in the 20th century which had four tropical storms or hurricanes simultaneously. Actually, an argument could be made that **in the 1995 hurricane season, there were FIVE simultaneously occurring tropical storms and hurricanes**. On August 29th, dying Tropical Storm Jerry was producing flash flooding over portions of central Florida as his circulation was spinning down along the east-central Florida coast. On that same day, Hurricane Humberto, Tropical Storm Iris, Tropical Storm Karen and Tropical Storm, soon-to-be-Hurricane Luis were in the North Atlantic Basin. Moreover, the remnants of what was Hurricane Felix were moving into Scandinavia.

Because of Humberto's large size and circulation, he absorbed and effectively eliminated the much weaker and smaller Iris. When there are three or more tropical cyclones in close proximity to each other, and all are strong, they have been observed to rotate around each other like arcing dumbbells. This is known as the **Fujiwara Effect**, named after the individual who observed the phenomenon in the western Pacific with multiple powerful typhoons.

Thus, the stronger the winds of the hurricane/typhoon, the less likely is it to be sheared to weakening by, or and/or absorbed by, another hurricane/typhoon. Rather, the systems "barbell" around each other.

Just how strong can a hurricane's winds become? It appears that an upper limit is likely, based on empirical data and the genesis-cycle of the storm. We observe that as the hurricane goes through an intensification process, its eye, about which is the storm's circulation, shrinks. In some of the most powerful hurricanes and typhoons, the eyes have shrunk to fewer than ten miles, with about 5 miles being the most compact eye yet observed.

In superhurricanes such as the 1935 Florida Keys Hurricane, 1955's Janet, 1969's Camille, 1980's Allen and 1988's Gilbert, sustained winds exceeded 175 miles per hour. In Janet, winds were about 200 mph, and in Camille, winds were estimated to have been at from 190 mph to 200 mph, perhaps to 210 mph, when she made landfall on the Mississippi coast. Note that all the monster hurricanes either formed in the very warm Gulf of Mexico or moved into the Gulf. This truly puts the Gulf states at greatest risk for being hit by the worst possible hurricanes.

These winds are the sustained one-minute average maximum winds. There are also gusts that can exceed the sustained winds by 20 or more mph.

Thus, based on this record, it may be that the greatest sustained winds physically possible in a hurricane are from 200 to 230 mph. This would be the extreme....threatening the 231 mph world's record at the summit Mount Washington, New Hampshire.

How do such high winds affect a person caught outside in them? This writer made the pilgrimage to Mt. Washington, which is what everyone who enjoys weather...is a weather buff...is encouraged to do at least once in your lifetime. I took the cog railway up the mountain to the summit when the common occurrence of having sustained winds of at least 100 miles per hour was occurring. (This intensity wind is more common during the colder half of the year, when weather systems are stronger.) I climbed to the top of the heap of rocks which marked the summit and tried to stand in sustained winds of over 100 mph. It was impossible. Fortunately, there are no trees or other objects that could be hurled as missiles by the wind up there. I had to gingerly climb down from the mountain top on my hands and knees, and then made it to the weather observatory for sanctuary. Thinking about it now, and viewing the videotape of the event, makes for a quite humorous event. However, in a hurricane closer to sea-level with such wind hurling trash cans, tree limbs, parts of roofing, glass, etc., this situation would be life-threatening.

I quote from a booklet by the National Hurricane Center, entitled, "HURRICANE! - A Familiarization Booklet":

"As winds increase, pressure against objects is added at a disproportionate rate. Pressure force against a wall mounts with the square of wind speed so that a threefold increase in windspeed gives a ninefold increase in pressure. Thus, a 25 mph wind causes about 1.6 pounds of pressure per square foot. A four-by-eight sheet of plywood will be pushed by a force of 50 pounds. In 75 mph winds, that force becomes 450 pounds, and in 125 mph, it becomes 1,250 pounds. For some structures, this force is enough to cause failure."

Here is another way to look at the force of the wind. If you hold your hand outside a car window with the car moving at 70 mph, your hand is feeling one-fourth of the force of 140 mph winds. The wind force increases four times because of squaring the two speeds.

If you try to walk into a 70 mph wind, you would have to lean at about a 45-degree angle to not be blown down to the ground.

When the winds reach 80 to 100 mph, it is impossible to walk into it unless you are holding on to a railing or some other support.

In 120 mph winds, objects that are becoming missiles, such as a tree limb, trash can or lawn chair, can kill you when the wind blows the object into your body.

An average person who tries to stand outside in a wind of at lest 130 miles per hour would be lifted off the ground.

A 160 mph wind is equal to 600 pounds of drag force.

Consider what happened to a woman who tried to ride out Hurricane Andrew of 1992 in her home in south Florida. The following several paragraphs are reproduced from our book entitled, "TERROR FROM THE SKIES!", by this author, which contains stories of severe and unusual weather. This account is written in the first person as a personal experience.

"At the end of the 20th century, more horror stories resulted from hurricane destruction. In 1992, Hurricane Andrew tore across the southern tip of Florida, sparing Miami from the worst but devastating Homestead and vicinity.

"Shortly after the event, I was in Miami participating with colleague meteorologists in a weather symposium on warning and preparedness. I went with colleagues from the National Hurricane Center to tour the destruction caused by Hurricane Andrew. Although the destroyed homes and other buildings were shocking, one story from that storm particularly remains in my memory.

"I visited a slab and some bricks remaining from one of the homes in the Homestead area. An elderly woman had lived alone in this house. During the fury of Hurricane Andrew, the woman's neighbors, who lived in a somewhat stronger house, begged her to come stay with them for shelter. She refused because she wanted to stay with and protect her cats in her own home. Winds that may have reached 175 mph blew the roof off that house and proceeded to destroy much of the rest, blowing away just about everything inside the house. The wind blew a two-by-four piece of wood through the woman's chest, but missed her heart. She lied there, on the floor, alive for about three hours as the storm raged and then subsided. Her neighbors then came to her, desperately trying to save her life. They could not attempt to pull the lumber back out through her for fear of killing her outright.

"Ironically, the only phone still working in the area was the phone which remained intact in the remains of this woman's house. The neighbors used it, but all the lines to Miami were busy. Even if they could get through, there were so many people needing to be rescued that enough helicopters were not available in short notice to attempt to save everybody. Roads that remained were littered with debris, so that it took time before much ground transportation were even possible. Then, after hours of horror, the woman died.

"When I walked in her house all I could do was realize as a meteorologist, even if I have an accurate forecast telling exactly where the worst hit areas from a major hurricane would be, that many people would try to "ride out the storm". Consider the hurricane party in Pass Christian, Mississippi. Consider the woman in south Florida who wanted to stay with her cats.

"Also, ironically, her phone was used to call LONG DISTANCE, such as to Chicago, New York and New England, where the lines were not tied up, to get messages relayed BACK to Florida to get help.

In Andrew, there was considerable destruction from the storm surge, but the excessive damage in this case was primarily due to the ferocious winds."

Consider two hurricanes moving at about the same rate. If one contains 150 mph maximum sustained winds and the other's is 100 mph, then the pressure gradient or difference from the edge of the rain shield to the eye is much greater in the more powerful storm. The central pressure would also be much lower in the stronger hurricane. A record of the barometric pressure would show a very rapid fall as the stronger hurricane moves across the area. Thus, you can correlate the barometric pressure and its rate of change with the intensity of the winds.

Following are some wind-speed records and barograph records from hurricanes as they (the eye) passed over or near the observation sites.

The eye of the Great 1938 Hurricane passed just to the east of New Jersey and New York City. That area still experienced winds around 100 mph. Here is the barograph trace from Sandy Hook, New Jersey, off Staten Island, New York.

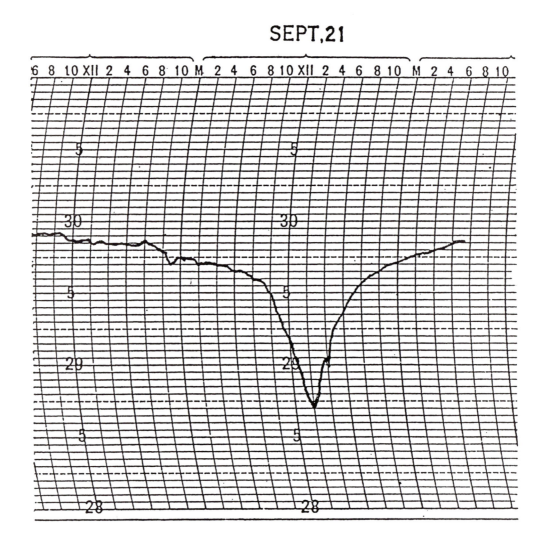

Figure 79. The barograph showing the record of barometric pressure at Sandy Hook, New Jersey during the passage just to the east of the Great 1938 Hurricane. Note that at 2 p.m. on September 21st the extremely rapidly falling barometer reached its minimum of 28.70" of sea-level pressure. At that precise time, the eye of the hurricane was about to cross the south shore of Long Island. Sandy Hook and vicinity, including Staten Island, New York, were experiencing sustained winds of 100 mph or more, but this was on the weaker side of the storm. (source: NWS)

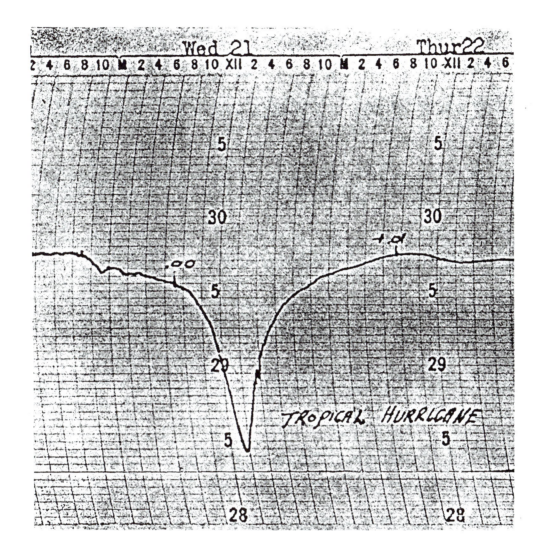

Figure 80. Here is a barograph from the then-Mitchel Field, New York, on Long Island, close to where the hurricane's eye passed over on September 21st, 1938. The V-shaped barograph trace is classic for powerful hurricanes. The pressure falls extremely rapidly as the eye approaches, and rises just as fast as the storm moves away, assuming the storm is moving at approximately the same speed and is not changing significantly in intensity. A powerful hurricane is more symmetrical than a minimal hurricane. Winds over central Long Island were at least 120 mph sustained as the vicious storm made landfall shortly after 2:20 p.m. local time. (source: NWS)

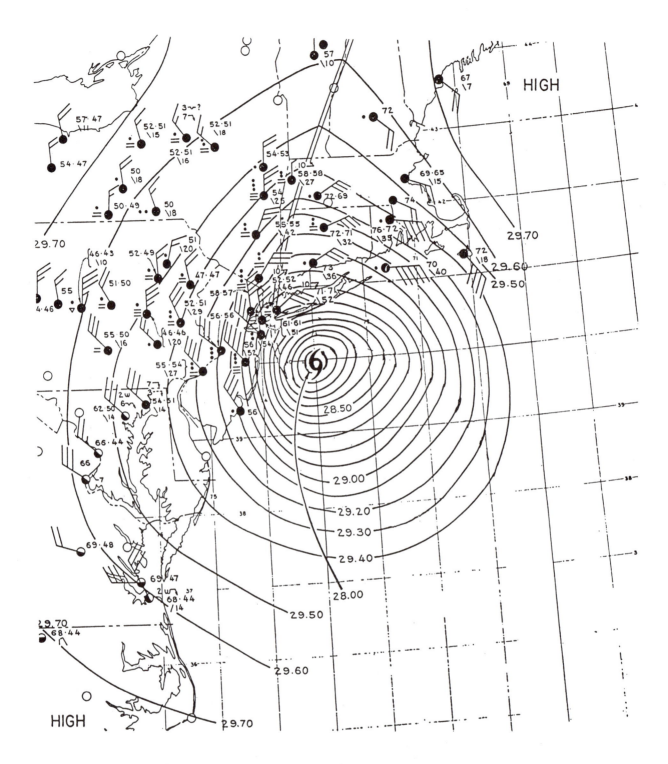

Figure 81. The surface weather map at 2 p.m. local time on Sept. 21st, 1938 as the powerful hurricane approached Long Island, New York. The storm then moved across Long Island Sound and sliced into New England, devastating Connecticut, Rhode Island and Massachusetts. The Blue Hill Observatory in East Milton, Massachusetts recorded a peak gust of 186 miles per hour. A thirty-foot storm surge put downtown Providence, Rhode Island under fourteen feet of Atlantic Ocean water. (source: NWS)

Figure 82. The barograph from New Haven, Connecticut, about where the Great Hurricane of 1938 made landfall in New England. Note how rapidly the barometric pressure fell between 2 p.m. and 3:30 p.m., almost an inch. More extreme pressure falls have been recorded in category 5 hurricanes.
(source: NWS)

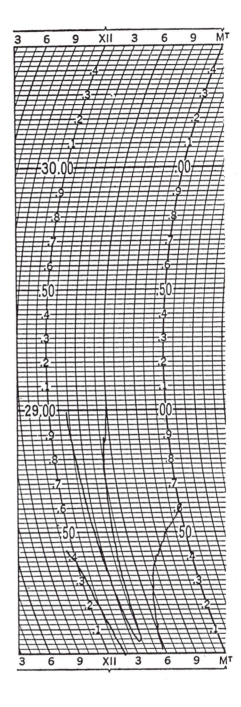

The simultaneous recordings of the wind direction, wind speed and atmospheric pressure give us another means for tracking the hurricane...this method involving surface weather observations. Comparisons of wind speeds and barometric pressures led to our learning the relationship between the two in hurricanes.

On the following page is an example of the wind speed record from a hurricane whose eye passed directly over the observation site.

Figure 83. The wind speed in knots as Hurricane Gloria passes directly over Cape Hatteras, North Carolina on September 26th-27th, 1985. To convert knots to miles per hour, multiply it by 1.15. Thus, the peak wind of 76 knots is 87 miles per hour. Note how the wind dropped below 10 mph as the eye of Hurricane Gloria passed over after midnight, and after eye-passage, the very strong winds resumed. (source: NWS)

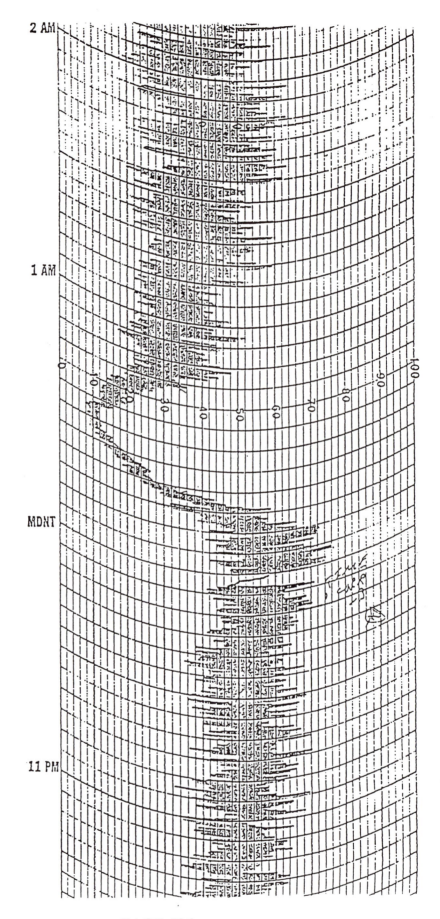

Figure 84. The winds and horizontal driving rain of a hurricane advancing on the Florida coast. (source: NOAA)

Most wooden homes are built to withstand winds of 100 to 125 mph. Stronger winds rip off the roof as its eaves become like airplane wings, and then further structural damage ensues.

The strongest winds in a hurricane are not at the surface; one study found that over the ocean, the greatest winds are about 1000 feet off the surface. After landfall, frictional interaction between the hurricane's winds and the land and objects on it reduces the intensity of the surface winds, which increases the vertical wind shear for a while until the winds at 1000 feet and above gradually are reduced.

Figure 85. People are killed and major damage results from a hurricane's winds, especially from major (category 3 or greater) storms. The storm surge, flash flooding and the occasional hurricane tornadoes are also threats to life, with the storm surge, discussed in chapter 12, usually being the greatest killer. (source: NOAA)

Attention must be given to the speed of hurricanes. To some extent, which is difficult to quantify, a fast-moving hurricane can result in stronger winds than if it were slow-moving. Slowly moving is 12 mph or less, and fast moving is 30 mph or more. If a hurricane has 100 mph maximum sustained winds, but accelerates to a forward speed of 50 mph, then the air it is carrying is moving at 50 mph. In at least one quadrant of the storm ahead of its forward motion, some of that 50 mph translational movement will add to the 100 mph hurricane's winds. An example of this is Hurricane Donna, which on Sept. 12th, 1960 crossed Long Island, New York at a forward speed of 40 to 50 mph. She had 100 mph winds, but sustained winds of about 120 mph occurred on central Long Island. The Great 1938 Hurricane was moving in excess of 50 mph when she crossed Long Island and slammed into New England. Her winds were on the order of 120 mph, but sustained winds were estimated to be on the order of 140 mph, and gusts exceeded 180 mph in southern New England.

In June 1957, Hurricane Audrey hit the Gulf coast near the Texas-Louisiana border, then accelerated northeastward, racing through the western part of Pennsylvania nd New York. Because she was moving at 50 mph and then faster, winds of 50 to 55 mph were being felt as far east as coastal New Jersey and New York City, even though Audrey was well inland.

Three years earlier, Hurricane Hazel made landfall in the Carolinas and then raced inland, passing over Rochester, New York. Because she was moving at greater than 50 mph, Hazel produced winds of up to 100 mph in the Buffalo, New York area, some 60-miles west of Rochester. Trees were downed on Long Island, New York.

THE STRONGEST WINDS EVER REPORTED IN A TROPICAL CYCLONE

The strongest winds in a tropical cyclone in the 20th century, as of this writing, were reported by the United States military's Joint Typhoon Warning Center on Guam on November 2nd, 1995. These winds occurred in Typhoon Angela shortly before she slammed into the central Philippines just days after Tropical Storm Zeke moved across the Philippines. Angela's winds were measured at 180 miles per hour sustained with gusts to 230 mph. **This 230 mph reading is the second highest wind speed ever reported on the earth's surface, being just one mile per hour under the 231 mph record at Mount Washington, New Hampshire.**

LARGE SWELLS AND RIP-TIDES

When a large and powerful hurricane is not a direct threat to land, passing some several hundreds miles away, the fetch of its intense winds can still have an effect on the coast by causing large swells to crash onshore. Moreover, rip-tides, also known as undertows, are generated. A swimmer frolicking in the ocean can be dragged by up to several hundred feet out to sea by an undertow, which is a strong current under the surface, moving away from the shore.

People have drowned from hurricane undertows. The person could be chest-deep in water when an undertow grabs you below and pulls you out a few hundred feet, perhaps dragging you under the surface. It is virtually impossible to swim against it, so the strategy for survival if caught in an undertow is to try to swim at a right angle to this current as you ride it out, and hopefully you can then swim away from it, and try to return to shore, hoping to not encounter another rip-tide.

11. THE EXCESSIVE RAINFALL OF A HURRICANE

a. rainfall amounts

Figure 86. Rainfall from a hurricane is typically excessive, because it falls from a large area of chiefly organized convection. (source: NOAA)

Typically, when a hurricane passes over an area, it produces from five to fifteen inches of rainfall. Amounts have been higher, especially in large and slowly-moving hurricanes.

If you are in the hurricane's rain shield, with the eye-wall approaching, the intensity of the rainfall increases. Rainfall rates of one to three inches per hour, and sometimes greater, are observed as the eye-wall approaches. Moreover, much of the rain is blowing horizontally in sheets because of the driving and extreme wind speeds.

A study published back in 1960 suggested that because of the extreme winds, much of the rainfall is not caught in a rain gauge. The study estimated that perhaps not even half of the rainfall is actually measured when the sustained wind speed exceeds 56 mph. Another study, published in 1982, which compared rainfall estimates by radar to what was measured in the rain gauges, concluded that the rain gauges recorded only about one-half of what was estimated by the rainfall-reflectivity estimates.

Figure 87. Some maximum observed rainfalls in the United States. All of these are the result of convection, some being from tropical cyclones.

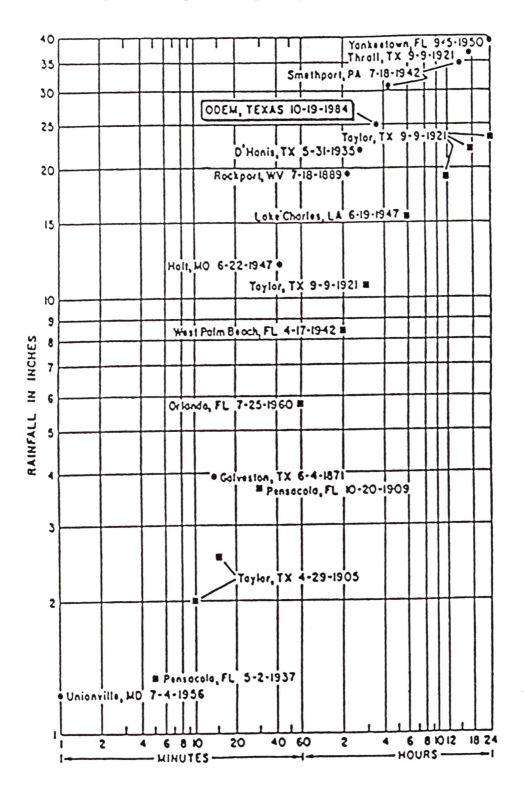

The most excessive rainfalls come from convective systems because only convective clouds...cumulonimbus-type clouds...are tall enough at say 40,000 to 60,000 feet for healthy convection, to hold sufficient moisture to deliver excessive rainfall. This brings our discussion to the problem of flash flooding caused by tropical storms and hurricanes.

b. flash flooding

Figure 88. Hurricane Camille, after moving well inland, produced this flash flooding on the James River at Richmond, Virginia in August 1969. Even after a hurricane has lost its powerful winds and has moved well inland, it can still generate excessive rainfall and flash flooding. Camille produced some thirty inches of rain in about 6 hours over portions of West Virginia and western Virginia, and killed more people from her floods that she did from her storm surge and winds along the central Gulf of Mexico coast where she made landfall. (source: Virginia Department of Highways)

Although five to fifteen inches of rainfall is typical from a hurricane passing through, much higher amounts have occurred from slowly-moving tropical cyclones, even after they have reduced to tropical depression status when well inland.

Along the Atlantic and Gulf coasts of the U.S., average monthly rainfalls are typically in the 3-to-5-inch range. Inland amounts tend to be lower. Thus, if the remnants of hurricane pass over a region slowly, a typical monthly amount can be exceeded in a few hours.

In June of 1972 this meteorologist was stationed at the National Weather Service Office at Binghamton, New York when Hurricane Agnes, a minimal category 1 hurricane, took a left-hand turn in the New York City area and then remained quasi-stationary over the New York-Pennsylvania border just south of Elmira, New York, which is about 60 miles west of Binghamton.

When the track-plotting of Agnes' path showed the obvious turn to the west, I issued a flash flood warning for the area, urging interests in the flood-prone regions to take appropriate actions including evacuation. But even I was amazed at the extent of the resultant flooding from some 2½ days of heavy rainfall, on the order of 15 inches, nearly a half-year's average. The Susquehanna, Chemung and other rivers rapidly flooded. All streams were out of their banks.

When the Susquehanna River was overflowing in the Wilkes-Barre, Pennsylvania area, it scooped up bodies from a cemetery, and some of these were initially inadvertently added to the death toll from Agnes.

I watched a Volkswagen Beetle floating down the Susquehanna River through Vestal, New York, a Binghamton suburb, with a bird resting on it. The water was moving at about 35 mph.

When I drove down highway 17 to Elmira as the waters receded, I noticed whole trees that had floated up onto the highway. In downtown Elmira, the streets were covered with mud over one-foot deep, and the high water marks were plainly visible on the second stories of buildings.

Even today, if you visit the Corning Glass Works factory in that area, in Corning, New York, a band of tape marks the height on the second story of where the Chemung River crested as it flowed through the factory.

Hurricane Agnes, even though she was a minimal hurricane...barely a category 1...was one of the most costly natural disasters to ever occur in the United States, due almost entirely to the flash flooding it produced. Hurricane Camille, however, was a superhurricane, a category 5 storm with 200 mph sustained winds. Although Camille caused devastation in Mississippi because of her winds and a 27-foot storm surge with waves up to 15 feet high on top of the storm surge, the highest death toll came from West Virginia and western Virginia, where Camille, although well inland, produced up to some 30 inches of rain in about six hours. Every river and stream in that region was out of its banks and many people were either swept to their deaths by the water or otherwise drowned.

Thus, even after a hurricane has diminished and is well inland, it can be capable of producing torrential rainfall resulting in flash flooding. According to the Federal Emergency Management Agency (FEMA), the greatest percentage of people who die in flash floods die by trying to drive their car through water that is moving and is from a stream or river that is overflowing. If the water is flowing, at typically some 30 to 35 mph, it need be only half-way up the hub-caps or wheel-covers to overturn even a large vehicle.

In recent years, we have learned that when the remnants of hurricanes move into an area with a concentration of warm, moist air, then the storm feeds on that energy source to produce excessive convective rains. A concentration of warm moist air is called a THETA-E RIDGE, which is explained in chapter 15.

Moreover, satellite and radar imageries suggest that many hurricane remnants go through a "breathing-in, breathing-out" cycle during the nighttime and daytime, respectively. That is, at night, the rainfall area "sucks in", becoming more concentrated, with the rainfall intensifying, and during the daytime, the remnants "breathe out", or expand, but the rainfall becomes more diffuse, not as intense. One possible reason for this is that the tops of hurricane convection are typically 40,000 to 50,000 feet high, whereas other forms of organized convection can be higher, and after sunset the tops may lower some as the heating of the day to enhance thunderstorm updrafts ends; then, radiative cooling into space from the tops of the hurricane-remnants' clouds destabilizes the upper troposphere, which later at night allows the convection to grow higher, which increases the rainfall-making ability and efficiency of the remnants.

Such was observed when Eastern Pacific Hurricane Tico crossed Mexico and moved through Oklahoma in 1983, producing one of the greatest flash floods in Oklahoma's history. One comment at the time from a meteorologist colleague who was flying over the area then was, "Oklahoma looked like one big lake with many islands."

Also, as the hurricane's remains move through the middle latitudes, the rainfall may be enhanced through interaction with other weather systems, such as a strong cold front. We may yet see this interesting event occur: a late-season hurricane moves into the northeast U.S. as an early-season surge of cold air also arrives, resulting in five to ten inches of rain along the coast, but five to ten feet of snow inland. Imagine the drifts with hurricane-force winds.

A study by J. Parrish et al. published in 1982 offered the following:

<u>Some identifying factors for the heaviest rainfall potentials from a hurricane:</u>

●A well-organized pattern and large extent of the satellite-observed cirriform canopy indicate that the hurricane is likely an efficient heavy rain producer.

●Generally, the slower the hurricane moves, the greater the rainfall in areas under the rain shield.

●Topography over which the hurricane is passing can affect the rainfall amounts. (For example, orographic lifting in mountainous terrain can enhance the rainfall because the moisture-laden air is forced to rise, condensing more rainfall from the clouds. Superhurricane Camille's deluge over the mountains of West Virginia and western Virginia is a classic example.)

●Observations show that the heaviest rain usually occurs in the right-front quadrant of the hurricane relative to its track.

Although the winds and storm surge are critical hurricane factors to prepare for and warn against, the flash floods produced by hurricanes must also be treated with a critical level of preparedness.

c. hail in a hurricane

Hailstones falling out of the hurricane's clouds are rare. Perhaps the wind is just too strong to permit the hail-formation process to come to fruition.

In a phone conversation with Dr. Robert Sheets back in 1987 when he was deputy director of the National Hurricane Center (he later became director), Sheets informed this writer that he observed hail aloft in only a few storms. Sheets flew about 200 hurricane hunter reconnaissance aircraft missions into tropical cyclones.

As of this writing, the only time hail was reported in a surface weather observation during a hurricane was for four minutes, from 1208Z to 1212Z on September 18th, 1989 at the international airport at San Juan, Puerto Rico during Hurricane Hugo. The visibility during the event was only one-eight of a mile with thunder and heavy rain, and winds from the north gusting to 75 miles per hour. This proves the value of having human beings take weather observations, augmented by automatic observing equipment.

12. THE STORM SURGE OF A HURRICANE

Figure 89. A storm surge inundating a coastal area. (source: NOAA)

A hurricane's storm surge is the greatest killer in a hurricane. A storm surge killed at least 6,000 people...perhaps as many as 12,000...in Galveston, Texas in September 1900, and killed upwards of some 500,000 people in Bangladesh in November 1970.

a. definition of a storm surge

The storm surge is a rapid increase in the height of a dome of water as the hurricane's eye approaches the shoreline. At sea, the much lower pressure in and immediately around the eye causes the sea surface to be raised up by several feet. As this dome approaches the coast with its much shallower water, the dome becomes higher. In superhurricanes, storm surges have exceeded 20 feet. In category 5 Hurricane Camille, for example, the storm surge at Pass Christian, Mississippi was 27 feet, with waves of some 15 feet high on top of the water dome. The three-story Richelieu Garden Apartment complex was swept into the Gulf of Mexico by that storm surge. A 30-foot storm surge from the Great 1938 Hurricane on the Rhode Island shore put downtown Providence under water up to 14 feet deep.

Some of the highest storm surges from hurricanes and typhoons are on the order of 30 to 40 feet. Moreover, at sea, waves in excess of 50 feet, which are wind driven and are not the storm surge, occur in the most powerful, large tropical cyclones. The extreme wave heights have reached 100 feet in powerful typhoons.

b. the causes of a hurricane storm surge

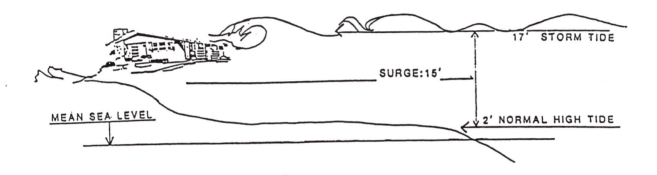

Figure 90. An example of a hurricane's storm surge. A normal 2-foot tide has a 15-foot storm surge, which produces a net storm tide of 17 feet.

The causes of the hurricane's storm surge are:

●the much lower atmospheric pressure in and immediately around the eye causes the sea surface to rise in a dome

●the fetch of the intense winds will force water in advance of the storm's eye to rise

●the dome of water rises rapidly...which can be several feet in minutes...as the surge approaches the shallower shore; where sea-floor level drops off rapidly from the shoreline, the storm surge is not as great as where the continental shelf is a gradual slope; the water swoops up as the dome moves over the shallower waters to the shore

●the best attack angle of the hurricane on the shoreline optimizes the height of the storm surge. For example, a superhurricane moving in just to the west of New Orleans would handily bury the city under 20 or more feet of water, whereas if the same storm makes landfall just to the east of the city, the storm surge may be only several feet.

People take shelter from dangerous winds, but if this shelter is along the coast, then even it may not save their lives from a huge storm surge upon which are battering waves.

PAGE 137

c. the effects of a hurricane storm surge

Figure 91. The storm surge from a tropical cyclone in November 1970 swept out into the Indian Ocean or otherwise drowned at least 300,000 people in coastal Bangladesh. A more recent estimate places the death toll at about 500,000. Many perished by being on islands just off the coast, that are only several feet above sea-level. A storm surge of 20 to 30 feet caused the greatest death toll in the 20th century from a hurricane.

The storm surge is not a wall of water, such as a tsunami which can be generated by an earthquake or volcanic eruption on land or under sea; rather, the storm surge is a rapidly rising water level as the hurricane's eye approaches land. Earlier in this book, in the personal accounts of people caught in the Sept. 1900 Galveston hurricane storm surge, the water rose four feet in four seconds, with a 20-foot storm tide.

As witnessed in the Galveston disaster and in the August 1969 Camille superhurricane, and especially in the November 1970 Bangladesh holocaust, people within several blocks of the coast can be swept out to sea. Entire buildings are destroyed or swept away. What the storm surge does not destroy, the fierce winds may finish off. And then there is the flash flooding to exacerbate the misery.

The storm surge is not confined to a small area. It may be from five to over 50 miles long up and down the coastline. Some parts of the coast will be harder hit than others.

To determine the height of the storm surge, one needs to obtain from the tide tables the height of the normal astronomical tide and compare this with the observed storm tide. The storm tide minus the astronomical tide is the height of the storm surge.

Typically, the stronger and larger the hurricane, the greater is its storm surge if it makes landfall. Over the ocean, the storm surge is created by the significant pressure drop associated with the moving hurricane and by the persistent intense winds blowing for several hours over fetches of at least several miles.

Since the storm surge is increasing as it approaches the shallower water at the beaches, and the moving water contains essentially the same amount of energy as it moves to the shore, the result is an increase in the surge height.

One study in 1982 found that the waves on top of the storm surge will batter structures along the coast and dampen out at some 300 to 700 feet inland.

Observations of hurricane storm surges show that the surge is worse if the hurricane is moving more perpendicular to the coast, rather than moving more parallel to the coast, upon landfall. The greatest storm surge tends to occur to the right of the landfall position in a slowly moving storm making landfall at an attack angle perpendicular to the coast. The height of the storm surge may increase by twofold or more when the track of a major hurricane causes the surge to funnel into a bay.

d. the hurricane storm surge and astronomical tides

The worst possible scenario for a hurricane's landfall is for the storm surge to coincide with an astronomical high tide. These occur occur during full moon and new moon, when the tide rises higher and falls lower during the tidal cycle. SPRING TIDE is the astronomical highest tide, occurring when the moon is in the full or new phase. During the first and last quarters of the moon's phases, we have NEAP TIDE, which is the astronomical lowest tide, which is when the tide does not rise as high or fall as low. Around the time of month when the moon is closest to the earth (called perigee), the tidal range is also increased: about two or three times annually during full or new moon we have the perigean spring tides, which is when the largest astronomical tidal ranges occur. The effects of gravity by the earth and moon play a major role in the ocean tides.

According to weather researcher R. Anthes (1982), the 1970 Bay of Bengal Bangladesh storm surge was up to 30 feet, and occurred at the time of high tide. The storm surge occurring at high tide vs. low tide obviously makes a difference in its height, but when it occurs during the time of spring tide, especially the perigean spring tide, then the worst possible scenario is underway.

Figure 92. A Massachusetts coastal community before being inundated by the dome of water from a hurricane storm surge. (source: NOAA)

Figure 93. The same community after the storm surge. Battering waves on top of the surge contributed to the destruction. (source: NOAA)

13. TORNADOES AND DOWNBURSTS IN A HURRICANE

Figure 94. As hurricanes make landfall, they often move into areas over which the atmosphere is moist and unstable. This can produce hurricane tornadoes. (source: NOAA)

Empirical data suggest that the likelihood of hurricane tornadoes is greater in intense hurricanes rather than in minimal ones. The tornadoes do not occur over the ocean, but when the storm makes landfall. After landfall, intense hurricanes weaken rapidly, with pressure rises of 30 or more millibars within 12 hours common. During this period, the tornadoes may be spawned.

To generate tornadoes, the local environment must be very unstable. Moreover, a hurricane coming into contact with a boundary such as a cold front may also increase the risk.

Studies of hurricane tornadoes have found the following. Most hurricane tornadoes occur in the right half of the hurricane relative to its track. This half, especially the northeast quadrant relative to the hurricane's path, is typically where we find the greater strength (right half) and greatest strength (northeast quadrant). One major study found that the majority of hurricane-spawned tornadoes are concentrated in the area between 30° and 120° relative to the hurricane's track, and from 100 to 250 miles from the storm center.

Yet another study found that the greatest concentration of hurricane tornadoes is the right-front quadrant of the storm relative to its path, and just outside the area of hurricane-force winds. Thus, winds of hurricane intensity may be too strong to permit the twisting spiralling updrafts that generate tornadoes. However, a colleague who lived through 200 mph Superhurricane Camille as she passed Biloxi, Mississippi, told this writer that he witnessed and heard at least one tornado during the height of the storm. The roof had come off his building and the rest of the structure was being demolished, so he went outside to try to find sturdier shelter. As he was holding onto a lamppost or similar structure while drenched and trying to survive the fury of the hurricane, he looked up and saw a tornado traverse just past him. The sound of the sudden increase in wind speed was also heard. Thus, there may be occasions close to the eye-wall in intense hurricanes, when tornadoes can be generated; however, the data suggest that most hurricane tornadoes occur just outside the area of hurricane-intensity winds.

Yet another study of hurricane tornadoes found that most of them occurred about 115 miles from the coast. Moreover, there were large wind-speed shears between the surface and about 5000 feet up; i.e., the wind speed increased significantly from the surface to 5000 feet.

A hurricane named Beulah demonstrated an exception to the above-found data. Most of Beulah's tornadoes were spawned in the southwest quadrant of the storm relative to its movement.

Hurricane tornadoes occur over land rather than water because of perhaps an additional factor known as frictional convergence. As the hurricane moves onshore, the fast-moving air hits terrain and structures, which cause the air parcels to pile-up (converge) and then rise over the objects in their way. The enhanced lifting, known as frictional convergence, may contribute to tornado-genesis.

Two other independent studies found that hurricane tornadoes are often associated with the strongest convective elements of the spiral rain bands. According to T. Fujita, downbursts also occur in these strong convective areas. A downburst is a concentrated downdraft of high-speed air that has been accelerating downward through some depth of the storm cloud. A 100 mph hurricane can, e.g., produce a 150 mph downburst of wind.

A radar image of a tornado was detected on the wall-cloud of Hurricane Frederic of 1979 as he moved inland on the Gulf coast.

Yet another study suggests that tornado-genesis in hurricanes is most likely in convective areas where the magnitude of the vertical shear of the horizontal wind at low altitudes is the largest. This has to do with the tilting and converging of vertical vorticity. Vorticity is a measure of the spin of a small parcel of air, and can be mathematically divided into the spin about a vertical axis (horizontal vorticity) and the spin about a horizontal axis (vertical vorticity). Vorticity is caused by the directional and/or speed shear of the wind in the horizontal and in the vertical.

Hurricane tornadoes are shorter-lived than their Great Plains siblings, and they tend to occur in bunches.

A study by J. Parrish (1982) found that even without tornadoes, the areas with the greatest wind damage tend to occur where the most intense rainfall rates also occur.

T. Fujita (1980) found that downbursts occur in some hurricanes, typically in the eye-wall and solid rain shield. By studying damage patterns which show that the damage directions are divergent by from some 10 to 20 degrees, the implication is that downburst winds are superimposed on the hurricane circulation. As an example, consider a hurricane producing a sustained 75 mph wind, with a 50 mph downburst superimposed on it. The resultant wind will be significantly above 75 mph.

A rule-of-thumb is that the force of the wind increases with the square of the wind. Thus, suppose the 75 mph hurricane + 50 mph downburst yielded the optimum 125 mph resultant wind in that locality. Then, the effect of the resultant wind is nearly three times greater than that of the 75 mph wind.

Suppose the wind were doubled. Then the effect is 2 squared or 4 times the effect of the original wind.

It should be noted that although the contiguous United States is by far the tornado capital of the world, and that not only severe thunderstorms, but hurricanes can also cause tornadoes, the U.S. is not alone in recording hurricane tornadoes. For example, on September 30th, 1995 Tropical Storm Sybil spawned a tornado in the southeastern Philippines that killed 18 people, including 7 children.

14. THE HURRICANE INTENSITY SCALE

CATEGORY	CENTRAL PRESSURE		OR	WINDS	OR STORM SURGE	DAMAGE
	INCHES	MILLIBARS (HectoPascals)				
1	≥ 28.94"	≥ 980 mb		74 to 95 mph	4 to 5 feet	minimal
2	28.50" to 28.91"	965 to 979 mb		96 to 110 mph	6 to 8 feet	moderate
3	27.91" to 28.47"	945 to 964 mb		111 to 130 mph	9 to 12 feet	extensive
4	27.17" to 27.88"	920 to 944 mb		131 to 155 mph	13 to 18 feet	extreme
5	< 27.17"	< 920 mb		> 155 mph	> 18 feet	catastrophic

Figure 95. The Hurricane Intensity Scale. (source: National Hurricane Center)

These groupings typically complement each other. For example, in a category 3 hurricane, the pressure is usually between 27.91" and 28.47" with a sustained wind of 111 to 130 mph producing a storm surge upon landfall of 9 to 12 feet. However, there can be situations e.g. in which a hurricane with a category 3 speed has a category 2 pressure; in such cases the worse category number is assigned to that hurricane at that time, since the categorization is based on the worst of EITHER the pressure OR the winds OR the storm surge. Keep in mind that if the sea-floor going out from the shore drops rapidly, the storm surge is not as great as when the continental shelf has a gradual slope.

The Hurricane Intensity Scale was developed by Herbert Saffir and Robert Simpson. Saffir was a consulting engineer in Coral Gables, Florida and Simpson was then the Director of the National Hurricane Center. Saffir and Simpson developed the Hurricane Intensity Scale in the early 1970s, based on observations of numerous North Atlantic Basin hurricanes.

DESCRIPTIVE DAMAGE FOR THE HURRICANE INTENSITY SCALE

Category 1 Hurricane: Damage is primarily to shrubbery, trees, foliage and unanchored mobile homes. There is no substantial damage to other structures. Some damage occurs to poorly constructed signs.

Low-lying coastal roads are inundated. There is minor damage to piers. Some small craft in exposed anchorages are torn from their moorings.

Category 2 Hurricane: There is considerable damage to shrubbery and to tree foliage, with some trees blown down. Major damage occurs to exposed mobile homes. There is extensive damage to poorly constructed signs and some damage to roofing materials of buildings, and to windows and doors. No major destruction occurs to buildings.

Coastal roads and low-lying escape routes inland are cut off by rising water about 2 to 4 hours before the arrival of the hurricane center. There is considerable damage to piers, and marinas are flooded. Small craft in unprotected anchorages are torn from their moorings.

Evacuation of some shoreline residences and of low-lying areas is required.

Category 3 Hurricane: Foliage is torn from trees and large trees are blown down. Nearly all the poorly constructed signs are blown down. There is some damage to roofing materials of buildings, and to windows and doors. Some structural damage occurs to small buildings. Mobile homes are destroyed.

Serious flooding occurs at the coast and many smaller structures near the coast are destroyed; larger structures near the coast are damaged by battering waves and floating debris. Low-lying escape routes inland are cut by rising water about 3 to 5 hours before the hurricane center arrives. Flat terrain 5 feet or less above sea-level is flooded up to 8 or more miles inland.

Evacuation of low-lying residences within several blocks of the shoreline may be required.

Category 4 Hurricane: Shrubs, trees and all signs are blown down. There is extensive damage to roofing materials and to windows and doors, with complete failure of roofs on many small residences. Mobile homes are demolished.

Flat terrain which is 10 feet or less above sea-level is flooded inland for as far as 6 miles. The flooding and the battering by waves and floating debris cause major damage to the lower floors of structures near the shore. Low-lying escape routes inland are cut by rising water about 3 to 5 hours before the arrival of the hurricane center. There is major erosion of beaches.

Massive evacuation of all residences within 500 yards of the shore may be required, as well as of single-story residences in low ground within 2 miles of the shore.

Category 5 Hurricane: Trees, shrubs and all signs are blown down. There is considerable damage to roofs of buildings, with very severe and extensive damage to windows and doors. Indeed, complete failure of roofs occurs on may residences and industrial buildings. There is extensive shattering of glass in windows and doors. Some complete buildings are destroyed. Small buildings are overturned or blown away, and mobile homes are demolished. There is major damage to lower floors of all structures which are less than 15 feet above sea-level within 1500 feet of the shore.

Low-lying escape routes inland are cut by rising water about 3 to 5 hours before the arrival of the hurricane center.

Massive evacuation of residential areas on low ground within 5 to 10 miles of the shore may be required.

TECHNICAL SECTION

The following three chapters are written for meteorologists and others with a background in meteorology:

---

15. USING THETA-E ANALYSES TO FORECAST THE POTENTIAL MOVEMENT OF HURRICANES AFTER THEY MAKE LANDFALL

It is essential to have a working knowledge of the operational forecast applications of the equivalent potential temperature (theta-e) in order to then experiment with its possible use in hurricane forecasting.

Since theta-e is used primarily to forecast the development of organized convection over land, and hurricanes are also a form of organized convection, it follows that studying theta-e analyses of hurricanes may prove fruitful for forecasting implications.

The chief use of theta-e is to forecast mesoscale convective systems (MCSes) and hurricanes are a type of MCS.

The approach this author is using is, for the next 15 pages, essentially reproducing chapter 39 from our book entitled, "WEATHER MAPS - How to Read and Interpret all the Basic Weather Charts", since that chapter fully describes theta-e, and then, after the lesson on theta-e, to discuss how it may be utilized specifically in operational weather forecasting to the problem of predicting how hurricanes are likely to move once they make landfall.

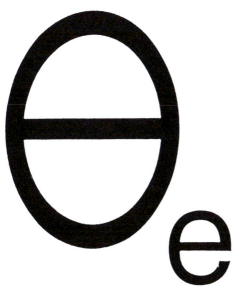

Figure 96. The Symbol for Theta-e, the Equivalent Potential Temperature.

One of the most significant breakthroughs in analysis and forecasting has been the evolution of the understanding of how to use the weather parameter known as the equivalent potential temperature, commonly referred to in meteorology as THETA-E.

Theta-e is a method of combining the temperature and moisture content, using the dewpoint for the measure of moisture, into one value, and then plotting these theta-e values on a map, analyzing them in order to find areas of concentrated high values of theta-e, and then using that information to forecast such things as flash flood potential, thundersnow and hurricane movements. Thus, correctly using the analyses and forecasts of the theta-e field are one of the biggest forecast advancements of our era.

Using what forecasters call thermodynamic analysis, parcels of air which originate at a specified level...typically 850 millibars east of the Rocky Mountains and 700 mb from the Rockies westward...are raised until all the moisture is condensed out, and then these parcels are brought back down dry adiabatically to 1000 millibars which is called the potential temperature reference level. Inotherwords, on a thermodynamic diagram or via a computer program, we take the current sounding data from a location, and go through the process of raising air from, say 850 mb, up to a level so high that by then all the moisture is "squeezed out of it" (typically around 200 mb in common computer programs), and then descending the parcel down to 1000 mb. At that point, at 1000 mb, we read the temperature of the parcel. The value it has is its 850 mb theta-e value.

In effect, we are combining the temperature of the parcel with the heat of condensation released as the air becomes saturated and then releases its moisture, and then descending the parcel past its origination point, 850 mb, down to 1000 mb.

The convention is to express the theta-e value in degrees Kelvin rather than degrees Celsius; therefore, add 273 to the Celsius value to get the degrees K value.

Now, the next logical series of questions is, "So what? What good is it? How do we use it?"

(continued)

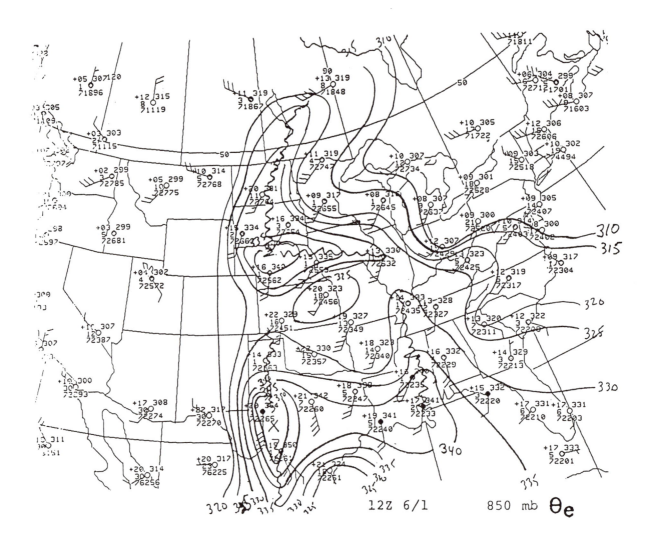

Figure 97. An 850 mb Theta-e Analysis. This is an 850 mb chart in which each location's 850 mb height value, in the upper right of each station plot, is replaced by the 850 mb equivalent potential temperature (850 mb theta-e) in degrees Kelvin (°K). For example, the 850 mb theta-e value for Topeka, Kansas is 323 degrees K.

This analysis was done by hand, drawing lines of equal 850 mb theta-e for every 5 K degrees.

850 mb theta-e ridges exist from Nebraska through the Dakotas, from Nebraska through Iowa, in west Texas, in the central Gulf states and a smaller one is observed in Kentucky-West Virginia.

All these ridges were inactive or "wasted theta-e ridges" at this time except for the one extending from the theta-e max in Nebraska east-southeastward through Iowa. In that ridge, some 6 hours later, thunderstorms formed. The surface moisture-flux convergence chart showed some one to two hours ahead of the convective onset where the first cells would likely form.

(continued)

These cells merged into clusters (with severe weather at some of the merging locales), and the thunderstorm clusters, continuing to feed on high-value theta-e air (which is a concentration of warm, moist air) then merged into a MESOSCALE CONVECTIVE SYSTEM (MCS) by 00Z, about the size of the state of Iowa. An MCS is a large area of organized convection, typically about the size of the state of Iowa, and persisting for 12 hours or more. The MCS that formed on this date produced a flash flood for eastern Nebraska and central and southern Iowa.

This case is typical of how to use theta-e ridges for forecasting organized convection (not single-cell type of convection).

Organized convection did not develop in the other theta-e ridges at this time because: the ridge north from Nebraska was in a region with a strong widespread cap inversion around 700 mb (the region was under a high pressure system with subsidence, i.e, with diverging sinking air), which inhibited convection even though the conditions for convective development existed (low- and/or mid-level lifting mechanism[s], moisture and instability); the air was too stable in the west Texas ridge; the ridge north of the Gulf coast was slightly active in barely unstable air; and there was no lifting mechanism nor instability in the ridge going over West Virginia.

Figure 98. Note the theta-e changes from the 12Z chart in figure 87 to the 00Z chart twelve hours later, below.

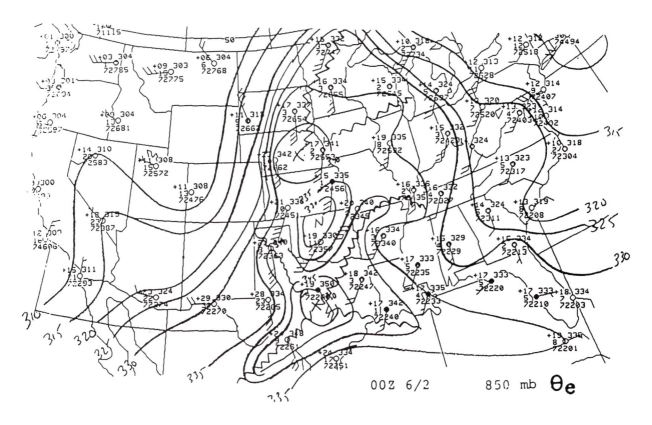

Notice how the theta-e patterns evolve and shift during the 12 hours between the 12Z and the 00Z charts. These changes are gradual. Therefore, because of the conservativeness of theta-e, it can be used to trace the warm moist air it signifies, from chart to chart.

At 00Z, organized convection was underway in Iowa and the theta-e ridge that was over the Dakotas 12 hours earlier had shifted into Minnesota into unstable air without a subsidence inversion aloft, and organized convection began forming within a few hours later over Minnesota in the theta-e ridge.

THE IMPORTANCE OF 850 MB THETA-E RIDGES IN CONVECTIVE FORECASTING:
When thunderstorms form in a theta-e ridge, these are the storms that merge and feed off the warm, moist energy supply which is high-value theta-e air (theta-e ridges are concentrations of warm, moist air). These thunderstorms therefore grow into a huge organized mass of thunderstorms and rain known as a mesoscale convective system (MCS). The crucial point about MCSes is that most very heavy rain events (3 inches or more within several hours) are caused by MCSes, so that most flash floods are caused by MCSes.

We now have an analysis and forecasting tool that can be used to anticipate most of the flash floods! This is a major breakthrough in weather forecasting.

A theta-e ridge, when acted upon by a lifting mechanism (e.g., a short-wave trough in the low- and mid-troposphere moving into the theta-e ridge) can be thought of as an axis of available potential energy that can be converted into kinetic energy of the subsequent convection.

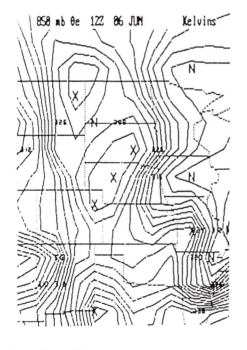

Figure 99. An 850 mb theta-e chart showing theta-e analyzed for every 2 degrees.

An analysis in 2-degree increments rather than in 5-degree increments (°K) permits a more detailed look at the theta-e field and helps to find side-lobes of theta-e, or side-ridges. Sometimes even subtle ridges or side-lobe ridges off a main ridge can become the focus for the start of organized convection when the conditions for convection exist within the side-ridge.

An example of a subtle side-ridge in the eastward-poking theta-e ridge into eastern South Dakota.

(continued)

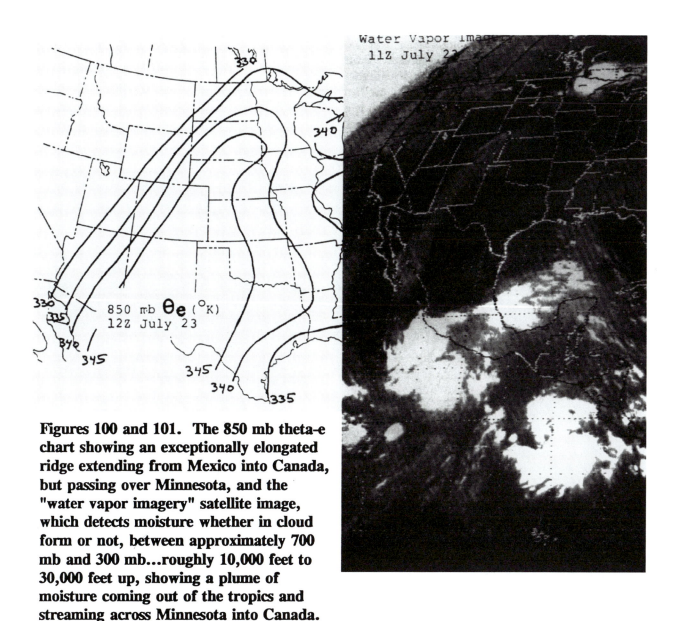

Figures 100 and 101. The 850 mb theta-e chart showing an exceptionally elongated ridge extending from Mexico into Canada, but passing over Minnesota, and the "water vapor imagery" satellite image, which detects moisture whether in cloud form or not, between approximately 700 mb and 300 mb...roughly 10,000 feet to 30,000 feet up, showing a plume of moisture coming out of the tropics and streaming across Minnesota into Canada.

This plume of moisture is called a TROPICAL CONNECTION. When thunderstorms form in a theta-e ridge, we know that we are likely to experience a mesoscale convective system, which is a very heavy rain producer...over 3" and frequently over 5" of rain...and therefore a flash flood threat, especially if the antecedent local soil conditions are already wet. The flash flood threat is enhanced when a tropical connection exists, with the tropical moisture streaming into the developing MCS.

(continued)   PAGE 151

There will be little moisture added above 500 mb in the troposphere, since the air is too cold to hold copious amounts there, but much moisture will be added from 700 mb to 500 mb, into the developing convection. Moreover, a tropical connection is a continuous infusion of moisture. Therefore, the impact of having a tropical connection streaming into the developing MCS is that it makes the heavy rain producing system an _even heavier_ rain producer. Many of the worst flash floods ever occur with MCSes which form in theta-e ridges and are accompanied by a tropical connection.

In our case study, now look at the 850 mb theta-e analysis twelve hours later:

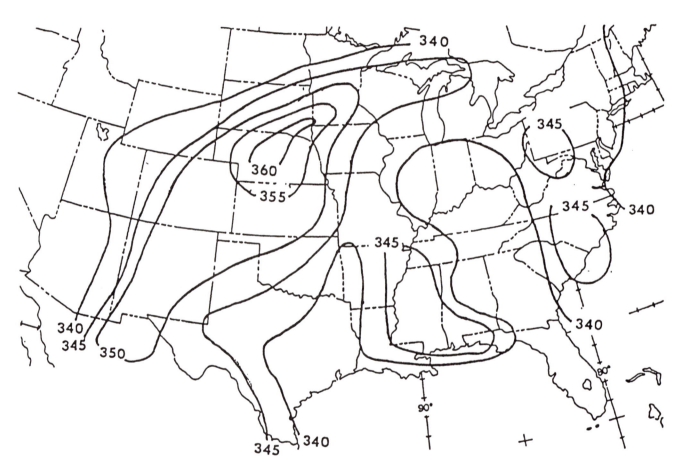

850 MB theta-e analysis for 0000 GMT, July 24

Figure 102. The 850 mb theta-e analysis for 00Z on July 24th. Notice how the ridge has intensified from roughly Nebraska into Minnesota. The result was that the convection that was over Minnesota some 12 hours earlier, intensified as it grew into an MCS, and the Minneapolis area received up to 11.1" of flash flooding rainfall.

(continued)   PAGE 152

Important Points About Using Theta-e for Forecasting Organized Convection

- An 850 mb (or 700 mb for western mountainous areas) theta-e ridge or maximum is not necessary to have thunderstorms; a theta-e ridge by itself does not assure thunderstorms; if thunderstorms do develop in a theta-e ridge, then they are likely to merge into clusters with the clusters then merging to form an organized convective system which we call a mesoscale convective system, MCS.

- If in a theta-e ridge and thunderstorms are expected, the surface moisture-flux convergence (SMC) chart typically shows where the first storms will form, namely, in or near a maximum of SMC or in a ridge of SMC, because the chief forcing for thunderstorms is in the lower levels of the troposphere.

- When an MCS is forming in a theta-e ridge, always check the water vapor imagery weather satellite image for a tropical connection into the developing MCS. This plume of warm moist air from the tropics seeds the convective system with additional moisture, resulting in copious rainfall and a flash flood threat.

- Whereas single-cell thunderstorms not in theta-e ridges tend to move with the mean surface-to-500 mb flow, or, for a first approximation, with the 700 mb flow, an MCS in a theta-e ridge typically moves with the 1000-to-500 mb thickness pattern except when the thickness lines diverge, which is called difluent thickness, in which case the MCS remains nearly stationary or propagates backwards.

- The MCS continues as long as the 850 (or 700) mb theta-e ridge is within the thickness pattern; when the thickness pattern (also called the "thermal wind") carries the MCS away from the theta-e ridge, then the MCS starts to die.

Other Uses of Theta-e Analyses and Forecasts

Although using theta-e charts as guidance in forecasting many of the heavy rain/flash flood threats is a major breakthrough in meteorology, various types of theta-e charts are used also to forecast some other weather events:

- heavy rain/snow in western North America

- thundersnow

- fronts aloft

- hurricane movements after landfall

(continued)

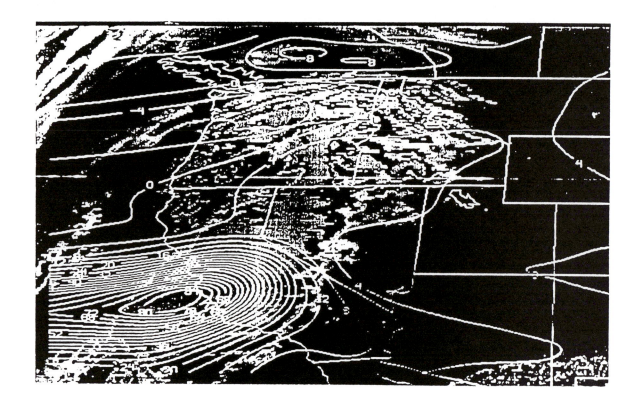

Figure 103. A 700 mb theta-e advection chart superimposed on weather satellite imagery.

For west coast heavy rain/heavy snow events caused by a major weather system, especially in the winter and spring, the 700 mb theta-e advection analysis and forecasts give rather good guidance in showing where the heaviest precipitation is likely to fall, namely, within the ridge axis or in the theta-e gradient just north of it. This technique works from central America northward, including Alaska.

An advection chart shows the change in theta-e for a time period, using for twelve hours with this type of usage. Thus, we are using not a theta-e chart but a chart showing the 12-hour increase of theta-e. A decrease of theta-e would represent drier and/or cooler air and would not be conducive to enhancing precipitation. What happens is that the cloud tops tend to grow higher in the advection ridge. There may be thunderstorms embedded in the steady precipitation but this does not necessarily occur. In or just north of this ridge the clouds do, however, show some convective development, growing higher than they otherwise would, producing more precipitation.

(continued)   **PAGE 154**

Using Theta-e to Forecast Thundersnow

Thundersnow is significant because of its heavy snowfall rates. When a theta-e ridge is superimposed on a synoptic-scale snowstorm, a potential for thundersnow exists. Although warm season convection is quasi-vertical, wintertime convection is often at an angle, and is referred to as SLANTWISE CONVECTION. The cloud tops may be under 20,000 feet high, but the convection may be 25,000 to 45,000 feet long, but occurring at an angle. A useful tool in anticipating possible thundersnow is a THETA-E SOUNDING.

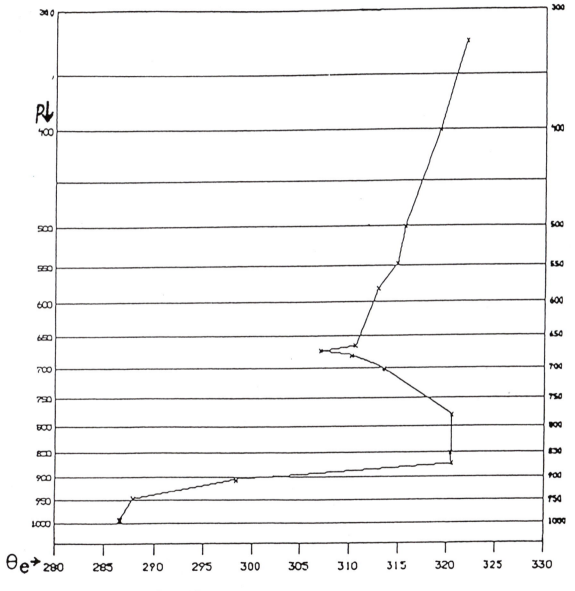

Figure 104. A Theta-e Sounding.
The vertical coordinate is millibars or could be the logarithm of millibars, and the horizontal coordinate is the theta-e value in degrees Kelvin.

(continued)

A theta-e sounding is constructed by taking the air parcel at each level of interest, such as for every 25 or 50 mb, raising the air until the moisture is all condensed out, typically to about 200 mb, and then bringing the air parcel back down dry adiabatically to 1000 mb. For example, to compute the 675 mb theta-e, go to the regular sounding and take the parcel up until all the moisture is condensed out (which we can do graphically on a thermodynamic diagram), then bring it down to 1000 mb at the dry adiabatic lapse rate, and plot its value on the theta-e sounding at the 675 mb level. Connect all the theta-e values for all the levels and analyze the slope of the sounding curve. WHERE THETA-E IS DECREASING WITH HEIGHT, THE AIR IS DESTABILIZING. If convection were to develop, this is where it would be originating.

The reason why decreasing theta-e with height is what we look for in the troposphere is because there are four ways to destabilize the local atmospheric environment to make the area more conducive to convective development: warm the air in low levels, increase the moisture in low levels, cool the air aloft and dry the air aloft. Any of these or a combination of these allows parcels that have been given a lift to remain warmer than the environment and thus keep rising to form convective clouds and their subsequent showers and/or thunderstorms.

From figure 103 we see that the atmosphere is destabilizing from about 775 mb through about 675. Convection, which typically starts at or near the surface in the warmer season, would start aloft, at around 775 mb, which would be about 7,000 to 8,000 feet up. This is an example of ELEVATED CONVECTION. Thus, we can have convection that is both elevated and slantwise.

Now that we know that when theta-e decreases as we rise through the troposphere we are destabilizing that local environment, we now need to determine if there exist a lifting mechanism and sufficient moisture so that we have the conditions necessary for convection: lift, moisture and instability (without a strong capping inversion aloft).

If we could generate theta-e soundings across the continent and then look at a cross-section of where decreasing theta-e with height is located and how this region is moving, we would have a guidance tool for anticipating the possibility of thundersnow.

The complex weather graphic on the next page is such a theta-e cross-section.

(continued)

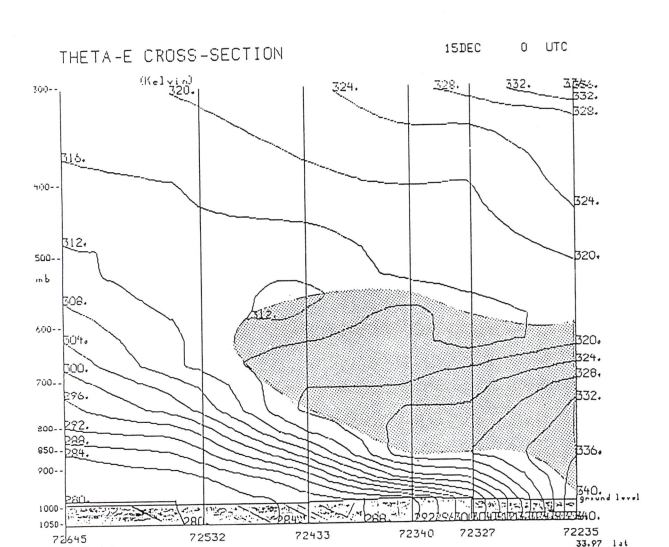

Theta-e cross-section supplied by James Moore, St. Louis
University, from their analysis program.

Figure 105. A Theta-e Cross-section. The vertical coordinate is pressure, in millibars, and
the numbers at the bottom are location identifier for weather stations. Notice at the lower
right is the latitude and longitude for a point in the southeastern U.S., and at the lower left
is the latitude and longitude for a point in the upper mid-west. Thus, the cross-section runs
from the southeastern to upper mid-west region of the country. The station i.d.s, such as
72645 for Green Bay, Wisconsin, are given to identify locations along the cross-section.
The theta-e lines from the theta-e soundings are labelled in degrees Kelvin (°K). The
shaded-in area is where theta-e values are decreasing with increasing height.

Thus, in this complex type of theta-e weather map, we see by looking at the shaded area,
where the potential for slantwise convection exists. The shaded area is moving upwards
and towards the mid-west.

(continued)

In this particular case, a major winter storm was affecting Missouri, and when the "nose" of the shaded area moved into Missouri, thundersnow broke out, resulting in several inches more snow than would have otherwise occurred from the synoptic-scale low pressure system itself. A video-loop of this type of analysis in, e.g., hourly or three-hourly increments would be quite useful to show the progression of this elevated area of instability.

Empirical studies have shown that the decreases of theta-e with height should be at least 5 K degrees, and when they are 10 K degrees or greater, significant convective potential is generated.

Using Theta-e for Fronts Aloft

Although most people are familiar with weather maps showing frontal boundaries on surface weather maps, these fronts also extend for some depth into the troposphere.

It is useful to look for fronts at 850, 700 and even as high as 500 millibars, because such an analysis can be useful in forecasting some types of convection.

When the air gets colder and/or drier at any level in the atmosphere, it lowers the equivalent potential temperature or theta-e for that level. Thus, the front, or leading edge of colder and/or drier air can be found at any level by looking for the leading edge of lower values of theta-e.

Here are two examples of when a front aloft may be a significant factor in convective weather.

Consider an intrusion of cold air flowing over the Rocky Mountains into the Plains. The cold front aloft at about 500 mb would cause cold air advection aloft, which destabilizes the mid- and upper-troposphere, and may lead to convection, or could cause stronger updrafts which lead to more severe convective weather.

Another example occurs when a surface cold front is advancing, trying to dislodge hot air. This is more common in the summertime when the hotter air is more entrenched and the cold fronts are typically weaker than in other seasons. So, the cold front is moving against the hot air but slows down because of the entrenchment and build-up of the hotter air. However, aloft at say 700 mb, the cooler air is still advancing. Ultimately, the front aloft overshoots the front at the surface. The leading edge of this upper front is the leading edge of lower theta-e values. By cooling in mid-levels, this destabilizes the atmosphere and sometimes leads to the creation of a pre-frontal squall-line of thunderstorms. Thus, there are sometimes situations in summertime when a cold front can generate a line of thunderstorms some 100 to 150 miles in advance of its location at the surface, and have another line of thunderstorms along the surface front itself. A theta-e cross-section every one to three hours would therefore be a useful tool for forecasting such thunderstorm potential.

(continued)   **PAGE 158**

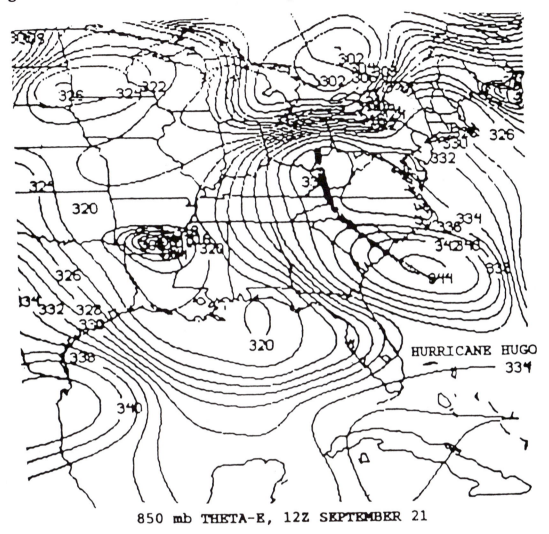

850 mb THETA-E, 12Z SEPTEMBER 21

Figure 106. The 850 mb theta-e analysis showing a pre-existing theta-e ridge from Charleston, SC to Charleston, WV, and Hurricane Hugo 12 hours before landfall, bringing in its own high theta-e air.

We know that organized convection feeds on concentrations of warm, moist air. These concentrations show up as theta-e maxima and theta-e ridges. Hurricanes are also a type of organized convection; they are a type of mesoscale convective system. We know that they form typically over tropical oceans in areas of high theta-e air.

When these tropical cyclones move inland, they lose access to their chief source of energy, the warm ocean surface and the warm, moist air above it. To maintain their heavy rainmaking ability, they seem to move into a pre-existing theta-e ridge over land, at least initially. As they move into higher latitudes, the strong westerlies...winds aloft...tend to take over as the chief steering influence for their movements.

(continued)   **PAGE 159**

In the Hurricane Hugo case in figure 105, note the theta-e maximum off the South Carolina coast. This represents the eye or center of the hurricane. Hurricane Hugo is moving inland, transporting its own high theta-e tropical air. This theta-e air must be distinguished from any pre-existing theta-e ridges near the landfall area. In this case, a pre-existing 850 mb theta-e ridge was in place from South Carolina into West Virginia. Although all the computer weather forecast models predicted that Hugo would hit the mid-Atlantic coast and then turn sharply to the right, striking New Jersey, the New York City area, Long Island and New England, instead Hugo moved into and through the theta-e ridge from Charleston, SC to Charleston, WV.

The theta-e analysis has been used since Hugo, typically showing hurricanes moving into pre-existing theta-e ridges. A notable hurricane-theta-e interaction was noted in 1992 when Hurricane Andrew crossed southern Florida, travelled through the Gulf of Mexico and then made its second landfall, striking the Louisiana coast. After hitting the coast, Andrew ran into a theta-e TROUGH, i.e., a concentration of low theta-e value air. Andrew abruptly veered rightward directly into a theta-e ridge.

In conclusion, the 850 mb theta-e analysis appears to be a useful guidance product for how a hurricane is likely to move during the approximately 24-hours after making landfall: **if a pre-existing theta-e ridge is in the proximity of the landfalling hurricane, then the storm is likely to move into the ridge initially.**

El Nino and Theta-e

El Nino is a sudden warming of a vast area of equatorial Pacific Ocean surface (and for at least some depth below the surface) water, in the middle of the Northern Hemisphere Pacific Ocean. El Nino may start in Southern Hemisphere waters off Peru and rapidly work its way northwestward into the south-central Northern Pacific Ocean. El Nino gets its name for the Christ Child, since it typically starts about November and peaks in December through March. (El Nino means little baby boy.) Sometimes it is referred to as ENSO, for El Nino Southern Oscillation.

El Nino does not occur every year. The El Nino event of 1992-1993 was especially interesting, because it persisted through the summer of 1993 and appears to have played a role in the disastrous mid-west floods of that year, because it created a tropical connection that persisted through the summer, with that continuous mid- and upper-tropospheric moisture injection feeding into persistent 850 mb theta-e ridges over the mid-west United States.

The cause of El Nino is unknown. Some type of dynamic heating process is suspected. Thus, El Nino remains a fascinating mystery of oceanography.

(continued)

When such a vast ocean surface warms up...sometimes by more than 5 Fahrenheit degrees, it warms the air above it. Warmer air can hold more moisture than when it was cooler; consequently, this warm air absorbs more water vapor from the ocean. Much of this moisture works its way up to mid-levels of the troposphere (700 to 500 mb), and some of the moisture is transported to the upper-troposphere (above 500 mb, up to 300 to 200 mb).

Next, we would want to know how the moisture gets transported across the Pacific into North America in tropical plumes. We know that tropical connections occur throughout the year around the globe, but when El Nino occurs, we have intense and persistent tropical connections, with major, continuous infusions of moisture from the tropical North Pacific into North America in the mid- and upper-troposphere.

There are two chief sources of this transport: the sub-tropical jet-stream and anticyclonic outflow aloft from organized convection in the tropics.

Jet-streaks of the sub-tropical jet readily carry the air and its moisture from the source region for this tropical moisture east-northeastward across the central and eastern Pacific and over the North American continent.

The other major source of this moisture plume is in the Intertropical Convergence Zone (ITCZ). There are typically large high pressure systems over the North Atlantic and North Pacific Oceans, and there are also large highs over the South Atlantic and South Pacific Oceans. The low pressure systems move through and around these highs. The circulation around a high is clockwise in the Northern Hemisphere and counterclockwise in the Southern Hemisphere. This results in air coming together or converging near the equator, with climatological statistics showing us that the greatest convergence is a few degrees latitude north of the equator. This is the axis of the Intertropical Convergence Zone. The ITCZ axis migrates some to the north and south, but stays north of the equator. Most hurricanes form in the ITCZ since it is a zone of converging, rising and very warm tropical air...thus, it is air of a high-value theta-e environment. Hurricanes form out of organizing convection which is an MCS, mesoscale convective system. Since air is converging and rising into the MCS in low and middle levels of the troposphere, the air must come out of the system and diverge aloft. It does so as anticyclonically-curved plumes of air, which also contain the moisture.

Thus, each of these MCSes in the tropics, including those that become hurricanes, generate their own tropical moisture plumes.

These MCSes form in regions of high values of low-level theta-e.

In conclusion, **when El Nino occurs, the tropical connections are more intense and prolonged, and if they stream into MCSes over North America forming in theta-e ridges, the heavy rain/flash flood potential from these MCSes is enhanced.**

SPECIFICALLY, USING THETA-E FOR PREDICTING HURRICANE MOVEMENTS:

Because more weather observations are available over land than over the ocean, it is easier to generate theta-e analyses over land than over ocean areas. Theta-e may be useful in hurricane forecasting as following:

● Separate the 850 mb theta-e envelope that moves with the hurricane from any pre-existing 850 mb theta-e ridge over land. As the hurricane approaches land, it tends to move into the theta-e ridge and maintains its heavy rain producing factory even when it has downgraded into a tropical depression low-pressure system. Although the hurricane and then its remnants tend to move into a pre-existing theta-e ridge, the system will likely be steered more by the mid- and upper-level winds as it moves into higher latitudes, especially from about 40°N or higher.

● In the absence of a pre-existing and well-defined 850 mb theta-e ridge over land near where the hurricane is heading towards, the hurricane's own 850 mb theta-e ridge is usually still useful in short-term forecasting. The ridge typically "pokes" in the direction towards which the system is moving. Thus, analyzing the storm's own 850 mb theta-e envelope of warm, moist air shows how the storm is likely to move for up to 12 to 18 hours.

The initial history of using the 850 mb theta-e analysis with a landfalling tropical cyclone shows the following:

● In 1989, Hurricane Hugo, which was predicted by the computer forecast models to hit the Carolinas and then move up the east cost into the New York City area and New England, instead moved into a pre-existing theta-e ridge that stretched from Charleston, South Carolina to Charleston, West Virginia. Hugo moved from Charleston, S.C. to Charleston, W.V.

● In 1990, Klaus and Marco merged, moving out of the eastern Gulf of Mexico as Marco. Although the models had the storm center moving east of the Appalachians across eastern Georgia, Marco went directly into an 850 mb theta-e ridge west of the mountains and gave portions of Georgia significant flash flooding.

● In 1991, Hurricane Bob travelled directly up a theta-e ridge off the east coast, directly into New England.

These were the only tropical storms to strike the mainland within that time-period, and the theta-e analysis proved helpful in all three.

However, only three cases are not a compelling argument. Successive uses of this type of analysis through 1995, demonstrated its practicality, In 1995, the path of Hurricane Erin was easily predictable through using 850 theta-e from the Gulf states into New England.

The heavy rains and flash flooding occurred as Erin continued to feed on high-value theta-e air (i.e., on a concentration of warm, moist air), as she moved through a pre-existing theta-e ridge.

MCSes forming over land areas in low latitudes and moving out over the ocean can become tropical cyclones. The MCSes can originate over Texas, Africa and Asia, for example. MCSes form only in theta-e ridges. Unlike air mass or single-cell thunderstorms, most of whose life-spans average from about 20 to 60 minutes, a mesoscale convective system persists for many hours, in many cases over 9 hours. Therefore, an MCS needs an energy source to sustain it, which is the concentration of warm and moist air which comprises the theta-e ridge.

When an MCS moves out from the land to over the ocean and the conditions there, as outlined in earlier chapters of this book, are favorable for tropical cylogenesis, then if the MCS holds together sufficiently long, it may evolve into a tropical storm and subsequently likely reach hurricane status.

Indeed, if you study closely the enhanced infra-red weather satellite images over equatorial Africa during the hurricane season, you observe that most of the hurricane seedlings that move into the Atlantic as easterly waves originate as mesoscale convective systems.

Moreover, as a tropical cyclone forms in the Gulf of Mexico, Caribbean Sea, the rest of the low-latitude North Atlantic Basin, the low-latitude Pacific Basins and the Indian Ocean, it mushrooms as an MCS before growing into a tropical storm, in most of the tropical cyclogenesis episodes.

The relationship of concentrated high-value theta-e air and tropical cyclones is therefore established.

16. ANGULAR MOMENTUM TRANSPORT IN A HURRICANE, IN ISENTROPIC COORDINATES

It is good to initially review the mathematics of angular momentum and how it appears in the isentropic coordinate system.

Absolute angular momentum per unit mass of air, M, is: $M = \Omega a^2 \cos^2\Phi + u\, a \cos\Phi$, where the first right-hand term is called the Ω angular momentum and the second right-hand term is called the relative angular momentum. The Ω angular momentum is the angular momentum due to the rotation of the earth, and the relative angular momentum is the angular momentum due to the zonal motion of air relative to the earth.

From Newton's second law of motion comes the following: changes in angular momentum happen through the action of torques (tangential forces possessing a moment about the axis of rotation). There are pressure-gradient torques and frictional torques.

On an isentropic surface, a sink of angular momentum will force motion towards the axis of rotation, whereas a source of angular momentum will force motion away from the axis of rotation. On a surface of constant angular momentum, heating forces motion upwards and cooling forces motion downwards.

We will treat θ distribution separate from M distribution and look at the intersections of sheets of θ and M.

Now, let us look at the hurricane.

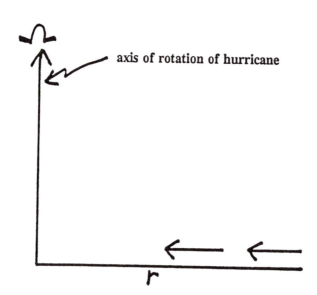

axis of rotation of hurricane

r

Figure 107. The axis of rotation of a hurricane and r, the radial distance outward from the eye. When air comes in, there is a frictional torque but no pressure torque. If we have a sink by friction, then we have a convergence of angular momentum (more comes in than goes out). In the relative motion, due to the decreasing radius, the angular momentum spins up. A torque is needed (which is the frictional torque) to get the air to flow towards the axis of rotation.

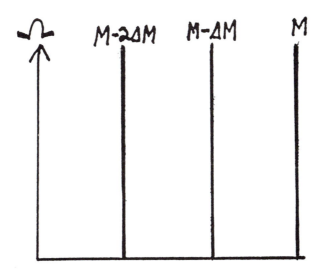

Figure 108. Even though the absolute angular momentum, M, increases with increasing radius, r, and decreases with decreasing radius, the sink dM/dt, by friction, has enough left over to keep it spinning, or in its early stage to develop it, i.e., to keep the system forming.

The hydrostatic assumption and symmetry assumption are being accepted for this argument.

In a steady-state hurricane, there is no mean pressure torque because of symmetry. Heating maintains the general circulation of the hurricane but it is coupled with the torques.

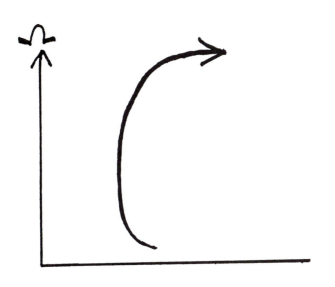

Figure 109. How does the angular momentum get out through positive values (increasing values) of angular momentum, and how do we get a positive torque in the upper levels of a hurricane? In the storm's upper levels, a convergence of the transport of angular momentum occurs, and the winds become supergradient (the Coriolis force> the pressure-gradient force), and the air flows outward. Therefore, in these higher layers there is a degree of freedom due to asymmetry.

In isentropic coordinates, a sink of angular momentum forces motion towards the axis of rotation; a source of angular momentum forces motion away from the axis of rotation.

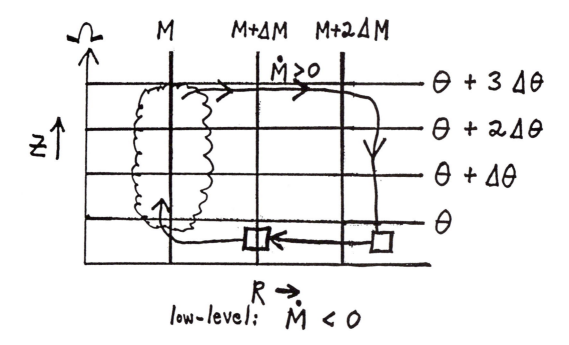

Figure 110. The sink will take away sufficient angular momentum from parcels so that as they travel from a to b, they are subgradient (the pressure-gradient force⟩ the Coriolis force).

Figure 111. $\partial M / \partial R = 0$. **The parcels are carried inward.** In a hurricane, these parcels come into the system in the boundary layer, picking up moisture and thereby increasing their equivalent potential tempera-ture (theta-e). They spin up through the stratified atmosphere.

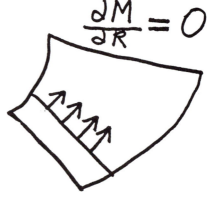

Also consider the heating. On a surface of constant angular momentum, heating forces motion upwards and cooling forces motion downwards. Sufficient heating in the atmosphere tends to cause upward motion along the angular momentum surfaces.

Returning to figure 110, notice that as a PARCEL comes in, it is losing angular momentum.

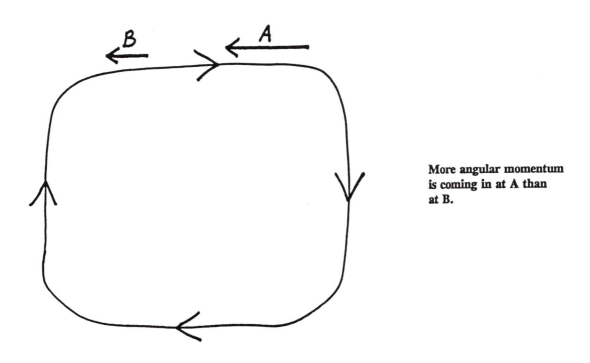

More angular momentum is coming in at A than at B.

Figure 112. A barotropic mode (a convergence of the eddy angular momentum transport) exists in higher levels of the hurricane...there, asymmetries exist. Due to asymmetries, other modes provide internal sources or sinks of angular momentum through the eddy processes, and provide heat through the eddy processes, all to change (to relax or anti-relax) the constraints.

17. COMPUTER FORECAST MODELS AND HURRICANES

(The reader is also referred to chapter 34 of our book, "WEATHER MAPS - How to Read and Interpret all the Basic Weather Charts"; that chapter is entitled, "Computer Forecast Models and their Prognostications").

For hurricane forecasting by the U.S. National Hurricane Center in Miami, Florida, three categories of numerical models are employed:

● the traditional suite of models run by the National Centers for Environmental Prediction (NCEP) at the World Weather Building in Camp Springs, MD, which is the group of forecast models run routinely throughout the day, and forecast models from elsewhere, such as some European global models;

● a moveable fine mesh (small grid spacing) model in which the storm is placed in the middle of the mesh with the model then run to determine steering influences on the hurricane or another powerful storm such as a major "nor'easter";

● a set of statistical models which store the records of past tropical cyclones and environmental conditions to determine probabilities of the current storm moving on certain tracks.

For anyone interested in detailed specifics on any of these models, you are referred to papers written by staff members of the NCEP and of the Hurricane Research Division. For the purposes of this book, an overview of each model category is appropriate.

THE TRADITIONAL SUITE OF FORECAST MODELS

These models incorporate the equations of motion of the atmosphere, known as the "primitive equations", and equations or fudge factors to account for such physical processes as radiation and friction, and equations for thermodynamics, and begin by forecasting a zero-hour (current conditions) forecast using the latest surface and upper-air observations with perhaps a short-term (few hours) forecast from the previous model run.

Each model forecasts in very short time steps of minutes, and yields forecast maps and numerical data that can be printed out for every 6 hours or 3 hours, for example.

Models that cover only say North America can not be reliable for beyond about 36 hours because they do not account for weather systems advecting in from outside the models' boundaries. True global models theoretically would be the best. They can be run for out to three days, with prognostications for out to ten days being useful for general long-wave atmospheric wave patterns.

Moreover, the definition of weather parameters typically improves as the analysis and forecast grid points for data are closer together, and with a higher number of layers in the model. A major problem of contemporary forecast models is that they do not parameterize convection and other mesoscale processes well, due in large part to the grid spacings being too large and the observational networks having too few reporting sites. Since hurricanes are largely convective systems, a form of mesoscale convective system, the contemporary forecast models can be used as a first approximation guidance in the short-term (up to 24 hours) for likely tropical cyclone movements but not for intensities. The worst possible mistake a forecaster can make is to accept with full confidence the forecast of any computer model for the future location and lowest millibar reading of a hurricane. If a suite of say five forecast models is looked at, no two models are likely to have the exact forecast for the hurricane for any future time period, since each model is constructed and initialized differently from the others. Thus, the output from these models is useful to look at for a possible first approximation forecast for the next 24 hours, but the forecaster needs to massage that information with his/her meteorological expertise and his/her knowledge of the biases of each model.

It is helpful to realize why computer forecast models generate errors and why errors grow. The initial analysis contains errors because of observational errors and having too few observations. There are phenomena on scales that are sub-grid. There are some approximations in using the governing equations. The physics are crudely incorporated. Most of the governing equations are nonlinear, which causes initial errors to grow in time. If most of the equations were linear, then probably most of the errors would be advected around but not grow.

Forecast models keep improving, but a good weather forecaster knows that sometimes, even if all the models agree, they can all be wrong.

MOVEABLE FINE-MESH MODELS

Employing a moveable fine-mesh model to forecast the movement of a tropical cyclone or other powerful storm is a creative approach to obtain additional guidance. This model is not global; it may be smaller than the domain of the North American continent and nearby waters. Thus, it is useful only for out to the first 24 hours to 36 hours of prognostications. The smaller the grid spacing, the smaller the forecast time step.

The approach is to center the model's domain on the storm, so that initially the system is in the middle of the analysis area. Then the model is run just like any other forecast model, and the predicted path of the storm and its pressure pattern is followable. Influences external of the storm will play a major role in the steering and evolution of the system.

STATISTICAL MODELS

Whereas the other models discussed are dynamic and mathematical, the statistical suite of models is empirical.

The tropical cyclone under consideration can be compared with the tracks and intensities of past tropical cyclones to determine the probabilities of the storm taking certain paths in the short-term and for out to 72 hours.

Thus, the hurricane forecaster combines his/her meteorological expertise with output from routine forecast models, moveable fine-mesh models and statistical models, in making the hurricane forecasts and issuing the watches and warnings.

CONCLUSION

Consider a storm with the following attributes:

●rainfall so intense that at its worst you cannot see across the street;

●winds so extreme that they can demolish houses and blow people down to the ground;

●a coastal storm surge that, in the extreme, can sweep people by the thousands into the sea;

●occasionally, tornadoes being spawned by the system;

●flash flooding as severe as from any other weather system; and

●a nearly-calm, usually clear eye about which the fierce winds and intense rains rotate.

Such a storm is the tropical cyclone in full fury, known around by world by various names: hurricane, typhoon, cyclone, tropical cyclone.

The goal of this book is to present all of these aspects of the hurricane and to incorporate some hurricane history into the discussion.

After due consideration of the scope of hurricane history, we are likely to come to this conclusion:

Surely, the hurricane is the most frighteningly majestic and intensely interesting of all storms.

Appendix A:

EXAMPLES OF HURRICANE WARNINGS AND OTHER HURRICANE PRODUCTS

Below are two examples of a TROPICAL WEATHER OUTLOOK issued by the Tropical Prediction Center/National Hurricane Center in Miami, Florida, for the North Atlantic Basin during hurricane season (routinely June through November). A similar product is issued for the eastern North Pacific.

```
TROPICAL WEATHER OUTLOOK
NATIONAL WEATHER SERVICE MIAMI FL
1130 AM EDT WED OCT 4 1995

FOR THE NORTH ATLANTIC...CARIBBEAN SEA AND THE GULF OF MEXICO..

THE NATIONAL HURRICANE CENTER IS ISSUING ADVISORIES ON HURRICANE
OPAL CENTERED OVER THE GULF OF MEXICO ABOUT 175 MILES SOUTH-
SOUTHWEST OF PENSACOLA FLORIDA...AND ON TROPICAL STORM NOEL LOCATED
OVER THE TROPICAL ATLANTIC ABOUT 970 MILES SOUTHWEST OF THE AZORES
ISLANDS.

AN AREA OF DISTURBED WEATHER LOCATED ABOUT 700 MILES SOUTHWEST OF
THE CAPE VERDE ISLANDS HAS SOME POTENTIAL FOR DEVELOPMENT.

ELSEWHERE...TROPICAL STORM DEVELOPMENT IS NOT EXPECTED THROUGH
THURSDAY.

PASCH


TROPICAL WEATHER OUTLOOK
NATIONAL WEATHER SERVICE MIAMI FL
1130 AM EDT THU OCT 5 1995

FOR THE NORTH ATLANTIC...CARIBBEAN SEA AND THE GULF OF MEXICO..

THE NATIONAL HURRICANE CENTER HAS ISSUED THE LAST ADVISORY ON
TROPICAL DEPRESSION OPAL...RECENTLY DOWNGRADED FROM A TROPICAL
STORM...LOCATED OVER EASTERN KENTUCKY.  THE NATIONAL HURRICANE
CENTER IS ISSUING ADVISORIES ON HURRICANE NOEL LOCATED ABOUT 850
MILES SOUTHWEST OF THE AZORES...AND ON TROPICAL STORM
PABLO...RECENTLY UPGRADED FROM TROPICAL DEPRESSION EIGHTEEN...
LOCATED ABOUT 1025 MILES WEST-SOUTHWEST OF THE CAPE VERDE ISLANDS.

ELSEWHERE...TROPICAL STORM DEVELOPMENT IS NOT EXPECTED THROUGH
FRIDAY.

PUBLIC ADVISORIES ON TROPICAL STORM PABLO ARE FOUND UNDER
WMO HEADER WTNT33 KNHC AND AFOS HEADER CCCTCPAT3. FORECAST/
ADVISORIES ARE FOUND UNDER WMO HEADER WTNT23 KNHC AND UNDER AFOS
HEADER CCCTCMAT3.

PASCH
```

Here are two examples of a TROPICAL CYCLONE DISCUSSION issued by the National Hurricane Center. This product contains technical information and the hurricane forecasters' assessment of each tropical cyclone underway. A separate Tropical Cyclone Discussion is issued for each system.

Initially, this product was issued for internal National Weather Service users and for interests in other agencies, but now it is readily available to anyone via the internet.

```
ZCZC MIATCDAT5
ÿÿTTAA00 KNHC 282050
...FOR INTERGOVERNMENTAL USE ONLY...
TROPICAL STORM IRIS DISCUSSION NUMBER  26
NATIONAL WEATHER SERVICE MIAMI FL
5 PM EDT MON AUG 28 1995

AIR FORCE RESERVES AND NOAA AIRCRAFT FOUND 78 KT AT FLIGHT
LEVEL...982 MB...AND A PARTIAL EYEWALL...SO IRIS IS NEAR HURRICANE
INTENSITY.  THE SATELLITE PICTURES DO NOT APPEAR SO IMPRESSIVE
HOWEVER.  MAXIMUM WINDS ARE STILL ESTIMATED AT 60 KT BUT IRIS COULD
BE UPGRADED TO A HURRICANE LATER THIS EVENING.  THE HEADING REMAINS
A LITTLE WEST OF DUE NORTH AT ABOUT 10 KNOTS.

NOT THAT IT HAS BEEN EASY SO FAR...BUT THE FORECAST IS ABOUT TO GET
MORE COMPLICATED.  THE AVN MODEL SUGGESTS THAT THE CIRCULATIONS OF
IRIS...HUMBERTO...KAREN...AND A PIECE OF JERRYS REMNANTS WILL DRAW
CLOSER TO EACH OTHER OVER THE NEXT FEW DAYS.  TRACKS AND INTENSITIES
ARE LIKELY TO BE INTERDEPENDENT.  THE AVN MOVES IRIS GENERALLY
TOWARD THE NE AND KAREN TO THE NW.  THE TWO ARE EXPECTED TO INTERACT
AND...BASED ON THEIR CURRENT INTENSITIES...IRIS WILL PROBABLY
DOMINATE.  THE INFLUENCE OF KAREN IS CONSIDERED NEGLIGIBLE FOR THIS
FORECAST.

RAPPAPORT


FORECAST POSITIONS AND MAX WINDS

   INITIAL      28/2100Z 20.9N  62.5W    60 KTS
   12HR VT      29/0600Z 22.2N  62.6W    65 KTS
   24HR VT      29/1800Z 23.7N  62.1W    70 KTS
   36HR VT      30/0600Z 24.9N  60.9W    70 KTS
   48HR VT      30/1800Z 25.9N  59.6W    70 KTS
   72HR VT      31/1800Z 27.5N  56.5W    70 KTS
```

<ZCZC MIATCDAT3
éTTAA00 KNHC 072040
...FOR INTERGOVERNMENTAL USE ONLY...
HURRICANE LUIS DISCUSSION NUMBER 42
NATIONAL WEATHER SERVICE MIAMI FL
5 PM EDT THU SEP 07 1995

SATELLITE IMAGERY CONTINUES TO SHOW A CLASSIC EYE PATTERN WITH THE
EYE WELL EMBEDDED WITHIN THE CENTRAL DENSE OVERCAST. THE LAST
MINIMUM CENTRAL PRESSURE REPORTED BY AIRCRAFT WAS 938 MB.
RECONNAISSANCE DATA SHOWS A DISTINCT DOUBLE EYEWALL STRUCTURE WITH
THE OUTER EYEWALL HAVING THE SOMEWHAT STRONGER WINDS AT THE MOMENT.
ALTHOUGH SOME INTENSITY FLUCTUATIONS WILL UNDOUBTEDLY CONTINUE AS
THE INNER EYEWALL WEAKENS AND THE OUTER EYEWALL CONTRACTS AND
STRENGTHENS...WE WILL KEEP THINGS SIMPLE AND MAINTAIN A HEALTHY 115
KNOT HURRICANE THROUGHOUT THIS FORECAST PERIOD.

INITIAL MOTION ESTIMATE IS 320/11. LUIS CONTINUES TO MOVE AROUND
THE WESTERN PERIPHERY OF THE RIDGE TO ITS NORTH. THE COLD
LOW CURRENTLY OVER THE NORTHEAST GULF OF MEXICO IS FORECAST TO OPEN
UP INTO A TROUGH WITH TIME...BUT WILL STILL HELP STEER LUIS MORE
TOWARD THE NORTH. THE TRACK PREDICTION MODELS REMAIN CONSISTENT IN
GRADUALLY TURNING LUIS TOWARD THE NORTH DURING THE NEXT 24 HOURS.
THE CURRENT FORECAST BASICALLY UPDATES THE PREVIOUS TRACK AND IS IN
GOOD AGREEMENT WITH THE MID AND DEEP LAYER BAM MODELS. OUR TRACK
INCREASES THE FORWARD SPEED OF LUIS AFTER 36 HOURS...BUT WE ARE
STILL A LITTLE SLOWER THAN THE GFDL.

LUIS REMAINS A VERY LARGE AND POWERFUL HURRICANE. LARGE SWELLS ARE
PROPAGATING OUTWARD WELL AWAY FROM THE HURRICANE. LONG PERIOD
SWELLS LIKE THOSE CURRENTLY OBSERVED BY NOAA BUOYS WILL PRODUCE
LARGE BREAKING WAVES WITH HIGH WAVE RUNUP. HEAVY SURF ADVISORIES
ARE IN EFFECT FOR MOST OF THE U.S. EAST COAST FROM FLORIDA TO THE
MID ATLANTIC STATES. HURRICANE GABRIELLE...IN 1989...WAS ANOTHER
LARGE HURRICANE THAT RESULTED IN 8 LIVES LOST ON THE U.S. COAST...
AND THE CENTER OF GABRIELLE REMAINED EAST OF ABOUT 60W.

THE GOVERNMENT OF THE BAHAMAS ISSUED A TROPICAL STORM WARNING
EARLIER TODAY. THE GOVERNMENT OF BERMUDA HAS ISSUED A TROPICAL
STORM WATCH EFFECTIVE AT 5 PM AST.

MAYFIELD

FORECAST POSITIONS AND MAX WINDS

INITIAL	07/2100Z	23.5N	67.6W	115 KTS
12HR VT	08/0600Z	24.8N	68.8W	115 KTS
24HR VT	08/1800Z	26.5N	69.5W	115 KTS
36HR VT	09/0600Z	28.5N	69.5W	115 KTS
48HR VT	09/1800Z	31.0N	69.5W	115 KTS
72HR VT	10/1800Z	38.0N	65.0W	115 KTS

Following are examples of **PUBLIC TROPICAL CYCLONE ADVISORIES**. The National Hurricane Center issues a public advisory for each system every six hours when the system is out at sea, and issues an intermediate public advisory 3 hours after the public advisory when the storm is close to or threatening land. As a hurricane is making landfall and starting to move inland, the public advisories may be issued every two hours. Individual weather offices whose areas of responsibility are affected by the storm will issue local Hurricane Local Statements with detailed information for the residents within their areas of warning responsibility.

```
MIATCPAT3
WTNT33 KNHC 270918
BULLETIN
HURRICANE GLORIA ADVISORY NUMBER 42
NATIONAL WEATHER SERVICE MIAMI FL
600 AM EDT FRI SEP 27 1985

...DANGEROUS GLORIA THREATENS NORTHEAST U.S. COAST...

HURRICANE WARNINGS ARE IN EFFECT FROM CAPE LOOKOUT NORTH.
CAROLINA TO THE MERRIMACK RIVER MASSACHUSETTS. A HURRICANE
WATCH IS IN EFFECT NORTH OF THE MERRIMACK RIVER THROUGH
EASTPORT MAINE. DISCONTINUE HURRICANE WARNINGS SOUTH OF CAPE
LOOKOUT.

AT 6 AM EDT...1000Z...RECONNAISSANCE AIRCRAFT REPORTED THE
CENTER OF GLORIA WAS NEAR LATITUDE 37.0 NORTH...LONGITUDE
75.1 WEST. THIS POSITION IS 50 MILES EAST OF NORFOLK
VIRGINIA AND 90 MILES SOUTH OF OCEAN CITY MARYLAND.

GLORIA IS MOVING NORTH ABOUT 25 MPH AND WILL FURTHER
INCREASE FORWARD SPEED AS IT NEARS THE DELMARVA PENINSULA
AND THE NEW JERSEY COAST BY MID DAY AND LONG ISLAND BY MID
AFTERNOON. A SLIGHT CHANGE IN TRACK COULD CAUSE THE
HURRICANE TO MOVE ASHORE AT ANY TIME.

MAXIMUM SUSTAINED WINDS REMAIN NEAR 130 MPH WITH GUSTS TO
150 MPH. TROPICAL STORM FORCE WINDS TO 70 MPH EXTEND OUTWARD
200 MILES NORTH...150 MILES SOUTH AND 170 MILES WEST OF THE
CENTER. THE CENTRAL PRESSURE IS 947 MILLIBARS OR 27.98
INCHES.

GLORIA IS A DANGEROUS HURRICANE AND HAS THE POTENTIAL TO
PRODUCE DAMAGING WINDS AND STORM SURGE FLOODING ALMOST
ANYWHERE FROM THE OUTER BANKS OF NORTH CAROLINA NORTH
THROUGH MASSACHUSETTS...DEPENDING ON THE EXACT TRACK OF THE
HURRICANE. COASTAL RESIDENTS IN THE WARNING AREA SHOULD BE
PREPARED FOR THE WORST CONDITIONS.

TIDES OF 8 TO 12 FEET ABOVE NORMAL ARE EXPECTED ALONG THE COAST WHILE
WATER LEVELS IN BAYS ARE EXPECTED TO BE 6-10 FEET ABOVE NORMAL. ISOLATED
HIGH LEVELS IN BAYS MAY OCCUR. DETAILS OF TIDES AND ACTIONS TO BE TAKEN
ARE INCLUDED IN LOCAL STATEMENTS BEING ISSUED BY NATIONAL WEATHER SERVICE
AND LOCAL GOVERNMENT OFFICIALS.

RAIN TOTALS OF 5 TO 10 INCHES ARE EXPECTED OVER PARTS OF THE WARNING AREA.

REPEATING THE 6 AM EDT POSITION...37.0N...75.1W. MAXIMUM WINDS 130
MPH...MOVEMENT NORTH 25 MPH INCREASING TO 30 MPH TODAY.

THE NEXT ADVISORY WILL BE ISSUED BY THE NATIONAL HURRICANE CENTER AT 8 AM
EDT.

LAWRENCE
```

PAGE 175

```
BULLETIN
HURRICANE OPAL ADVISORY NUMBER  28
NATIONAL WEATHER SERVICE MIAMI FL
10 AM CDT WED OCT 04 1995
```

...EXTREMELY DANGEROUS HURRICANE OPAL HEADING FOR THE COAST...ALL
PREPARATIONS TO PROTECT LIFE AND PROPERTY SHOULD BE RUSHED TO
COMPLETION...

HURRICANE WARNINGS ARE IN EFFECT FROM ANCLOTE KEY ON THE WEST COAST
OF FLORIDA TO THE MOUTH OF THE MISSISSIPPI RIVER.

TROPICAL STORM WARNINGS AND A HURRICANE WATCH ARE IN EFFECT FROM THE
MOUTH OF THE MISSISSIPPI RIVER WESTWARD TO JUST EAST OF MORGAN CITY
INCLUDING METROPOLITAN NEW ORLEANS.

TROPICAL STORM WARNINGS ARE ALSO IN EFFECT FROM SOUTH OF ANCLOTE KEY
TO VENICE FLORIDA.

AT 10 AM CDT...1500Z...THE CENTER OF HURRICANE OPAL WAS LOCATED NEAR
LATITUDE 28.1 NORTH...LONGITUDE 88.2 WEST OR ABOUT 175 MILES SOUTH-
SOUTHWEST OF PENSACOLA FLORIDA.

OPAL IS MOVING TOWARD THE NORTH-NORTHEAST NEAR 23 MPH. ON THIS
TRACK...THE CORE OF THIS DANGEROUS HURRICANE WOULD REACH THE COAST
BETWEEN APALACHICOLA FLORIDA AND THE MISSISSIPPI COAST LATER TODAY.
IT IS IMPORTANT NOT TO FOCUS ON THE FORECAST TRACK OF THE
CENTER...GIVEN THE LARGE EXTENT OF DAMAGING WINDS AND STORM SURGE.
WINDS TO HURRICANE FORCE ARE ALREADY BEGINNING TO SPREAD ACROSS
EXTREME SOUTHEAST LOUISIANA.

MAXIMUM SUSTAINED WINDS ARE NEAR 150 MPH...MAKING OPAL AN EXTREMELY
DANGEROUS CATEGORY FOUR HURRICANE ON THE SAFFIR SIMPSON SCALE...
CAPABLE OF CAUSING EXTREME DAMAGE. OPAL IS MUCH STRONGER THAN
HURRICANES ELENA...FREDERIC...AND ELOISE...WHICH AFFECTED THE SAME
AREA. SOME FLUCTUATIONS IN STRENGTH MAY OCCUR BEFORE LANDFALL.

HURRICANE FORCE WINDS EXTEND OUTWARD UP TO 145 MILES FROM THE
CENTER...AND TROPICAL STORM FORCE WINDS EXTEND OUTWARD UP TO 260
MILES. HURRICANE FORCE WINDS ARE EXPECTED TO EXTEND WELL INLAND
ALONG THE TRACK OF OPAL. HIGH WIND WATCHES AND WARNINGS ARE BEING
ISSUED BY NATIONAL WEATHER SERVICES IN THE AFFECTED AREAS.

ESTIMATED MINIMUM CENTRAL PRESSURE IS 927 MB...27.37 INCHES.

COASTAL STORM SURGE FLOODING OF UP TO 15 TO 20 FEET ABOVE NORMAL
TIDE LEVELS...ALONG WITH DANGEROUS BATTERING WAVES IS POSSIBLE NEAR
AND TO THE EAST OF WHERE THE CENTER CROSSES THE COAST.... THIS IS A
LARGE HURRICANE AND SIGNIFICANT FLOODING IS EXPECTED QUITE FAR TO
THE EAST OF WHERE LANDFALL OCCURS.

ADDITIONAL RAINFALL AMOUNTS OF 6 TO 10 INCHES ARE POSSIBLE ALONG THE
PATH OF THE HURRICANE. THIS WILL COMPOUND THE POTENTIAL FOR
FLOODING...PARTICULARLY IN THE APPALACHIANS.

ISOLATED TORNADOES ARE POSSIBLE OVER THE FLORIDA PANHANDLE...
SOUTHERN ALABAMA...AND SOUTHERN MISSISSIPPI.

REPEATING THE 10 AM CDT POSITION...28.1 N... 88.2 W. MOVEMENT
TOWARD...NORTH NORTHEAST NEAR 23 MPH. MAXIMUM SUSTAINED
WINDS...150 MPH. MINIMUM CENTRAL PRESSURE... 927 MB.

INTERMEDIATE ADVISORIES WILL BE ISSUED BY THE NATIONAL HURRICANE
CENTER AT NOON CDT AND 2 PM CDT FOLLOWED BY THE NEXT COMPLETE
ADVISORY ISSUANCE AT 4 PM CDT.

PASCH/MAYFIELD

PAGE 176

Here are two examples of TROPICAL CYCLONE MARINE ADVISORIES. This is an excellent product giving specifics about the storm.

```
WTNT25 KNHC 152054
TCMAT5
HURRICANE MARILYN FORECAST/ADVISORY NUMBER  14
NATIONAL WEATHER SERVICE MIAMI FL
2100Z FRI SEP 15 1995

HURRICANE WARNINGS CONTINUE IN EFFECT FROM ST. EUSTATIUS
NORTHWESTWARD THROUGH PUERTO RICO INCLUDING THE U.S. VIRGIN ISLANDS
AND THE BRITISH VIRGIN ISLANDS...EXCEPT FOR ST. BARTHELEMY AND THE
FRENCH PORTION OF ST. MARTIN WHERE FRENCH OFFICIALS HAVE ISSUED A
TROPICAL STORM WARNING.  A HURRICANE WATCH IS IN EFFECT FOR THE
NORTHEAST COAST OF THE DOMINICAN REPUBLIC FROM CABRERA TO CABO
ENGANO.

HURRICANE CENTER LOCATED NEAR 17.8N  64.6W AT 15/2100Z
POSITION ACCURATE WITHIN  15 NM

PRESENT MOVEMENT TOWARD THE NORTHWEST OR 305 DEGREES AT 10 KT

ESTIMATED MINIMUM CENTRAL PRESSURE  970 MB
EYE DIAMETER  20 NM
MAX SUSTAINED WINDS  85 KT WITH GUSTS TO 105 KT
64 KT....... 25NE  25SE  25SW  25NW
50 KT....... 75NE  50SE  30SW  30NW
34 KT.......100NE 100SE  50SW  50NW
12 FT SEAS..100NE 100SE  50SW  50NW
ALL QUADRANT RADII IN NAUTICAL MILES

REPEAT...CENTER LOCATED NEAR 17.8N  64.6W AT 15/2100Z
AT 15/1800Z CENTER WAS LOCATED NEAR 17.5N  64.2W

FORECAST VALID 16/0600Z 18.7N  65.7W
MAX WIND  95 KT...GUSTS 115 KT
64 KT... 25NE  25SE  25SW  25NW
50 KT... 75NE  50SE  50SW  50NW
34 KT...100NE 100SE  75SW  75NW

FORECAST VALID 16/1800Z 20.1N  67.1W
MAX WIND  95 KT...GUSTS 115 KT
64 KT... 25NE  25SE  25SW  25NW
50 KT... 75NE  50SE  50SW  50NW
34 KT...100NE 100SE  75SW  75NW

FORECAST VALID 17/0600Z 21.6N  68.2W
MAX WIND  95 KT...GUSTS 115 KT
64 KT... 25NE  25SE  25SW  25NW
50 KT... 75NE  50SE  50SW  50NW
34 KT...100NE 100SE  75SW  75NW

STORM TIDES OF 3 TO 5 FEET...WITH BATTERING WAVES ABOVE...CAN BE
EXPECTED NEAR THE CENTER OF MARILYN.  SMALL CRAFT IN THE WARNED AREA
SHOULD REMAIN IN PORT.
```

```
<ZCZC MIATCMAT4
éTTAA00 KNHC 101454
HURRICANE ROXANNE FORECAST/ADVISORY NUMBER   8
NATIONAL WEATHER SERVICE MIAMI FL
1500Z TUE OCT 10 1995
```

A HURRICANE WARNING REMAINS IN EFFECT FOR THE YUCATAN PENINSULA FROM
CHETUMAL NORTHWARD AND WESTWARD TO PROGRESO. ALL PREPARATIONS IN THE
HURRICANE WARNING AREA SHOULD BE RUSHED TO COMPLETION.

A TROPICAL STORM WARNING REMAIN IN EFFECT FOR THE EXTREME WESTERN
CUBA. AT 10 AM...1500Z...A HURRICANE WATCH IS IN EFFECT FOR THE WEST
COAST OF THE YUCATAN PENINSULA FROM JUST WEST OF PROGRESO TO THE
CITY OF CARMEN. WATCHES AND WARNINGS FOR THE REMAINDER OF CUBA AND
THE CAYMAN ISLANDS ARE DISCONTINUED AT 10 AM...1500Z.

ALL INTERESTS IN THE NORTHWESTERN CARIBBEAN...AND THE SOUTHERN AND
WESTERN GULF OF MEXICO SHOULD MONITOR THE PROGRESS OF THIS
HURRICANE.

HURRICANE CENTER LOCATED NEAR 19.5N 85.5W AT 10/1500Z
POSITION ACCURATE WITHIN 30 NM

PRESENT MOVEMENT TOWARD THE WEST OR 280 DEGREES AT 7 KT

ESTIMATED MINIMUM CENTRAL PRESSURE 972 MB
EYE DIAMETER 40 NM
MAX SUSTAINED WINDS 90 KT WITH GUSTS TO 110 KT
64 KT....... 50NE 50SE 50SW 50NW
50 KT......120NE 120SE 75SW 75NW
34 KT......150NE 150SE 100SW 120NW
12 FT SEAS..150NE 150SE 100SW 120NW
ALL QUADRANT RADII IN NAUTICAL MILES

REPEAT...CENTER LOCATED NEAR 19.5N 85.5W AT 10/1500Z
AT 10/1200Z CENTER WAS LOCATED NEAR 19.4N 85.1W

FORECAST VALID 11/0000Z 19.7N 86.6W
MAX WIND 95 KT...GUSTS 115 KT
64 KT... 50NE 50SE 50SW 50NW
50 KT...120NE 120SE 75SW 75NW
34 KT...150NE 150SE 100SW 120NW

FORECAST VALID 11/1200Z 20.0N 88.5W...INLAND
MAX WIND 65 KT...GUSTS 80 KT
64 KT... 25NE 25SE 25SW 25NW
50 KT...120NE 120SE 75SW 75NW
34 KT...150NE 150SE 100SW 120NW

FORECAST VALID 12/0000Z 20.5N 90.5W OVER WATER
MAX WIND 65 KT...GUSTS 80 KT
64 KT... 25NE 25SE 25SW 25NW
50 KT...120NE 120SE 75SW 75NW
34 KT...150NE 150SE 100SW 120NW

REQUEST FOR 3 HOURLY SHIP REPORTS WITHIN 300 MILES OF 19.5N 85.5W

EXTENDED OUTLOOK...USE FOR GUIDANCE ONLY...ERRORS MAY BE LARGE

OUTLOOK VALID 12/1200Z 20.5N 92.0W
MAX WIND 80 KT...GUSTS 95 KT
50 KT...120NE 120SE 75SW 75NW

OUTLOOK VALID 13/1200Z 21.0N 95.0W
MAX WIND 90 KT...GUSTS 110 KT
50 KT...120NE 120SE 75SW 75NW

NEXT ADVISORY AT 10/2100Z

AVILA   **PAGE 178**

A HURRICANE LOCAL STATEMENT is issued by the local National Weather Service office in an affected area by a tropical cyclone. It complements the public hurricane advisory with supplemental information for local interests. Below is an example.

```
SJUHLSSJU
TTAA00 KSJ1 181420

BULLETIN
IMMEDIATE BROADCAST REQUESTED
HURRICANE HUGO LOCAL STATEMENT
NATIONAL WEATHER SERVICE SAN JUAN PR
1030 AM AST MON SEP 18 1989

...THE EYE OF EXTREMELY DANGEROUS HURRICANE HUGO NOW MOVING WEST
NORTHWEST ALONG THE NORTH COAST OF PUERTO RICO...
...DAMAGING WINDS AND COASTAL FLOODING WIDESPREAD AS THE EYEWALL
SKIRTS THE NORTHEAST COAST...

...A HURRICANE WARNING IS IN EFFECT FOR THE U. S. VIRGIN ISLANDS AND
PUERTO RICO...
...A COASTAL FLOOD WARNING IS IN EFFECT FOR THE U.S. VIRGIN ISLANDS
AND PUERTO RICO...
...A FLOOD WARNING IS IN EFFECT FOR THE U.S. VIRGIN ISLANDS...
AND ALL OF EASTERN PUERTO RICO INCLUDING VIEQUES AND CULEBRA...
...A FLASH FLOOD WARNING IS IN EFFECT FOR CENTRAL AND WESTERN
PUERTO RICO...

AT 1030 AM...NATIONAL WEATHER SERVICE RADAR INDICATED THE EYE OF
HURRICANE HUGO CENTERED JUST OFFSHORE TO THE NORTH OF RIO GRANDE
IN THE NORTH COAST OF PUERTO RICO. THE EXTREMELY DANGEROUS EFFECTS OF
THE EYEWALL ARE POUNDING THE NORTHEAST COAST...INCLUDING THE SAN
JUAN METRO AREA.

WINDS ARE NOW SUSTAINED AT HURRICANE FORCE IN SAN JUAN...GUSTING TO
NEAR 100 MPH IN THE PAST FEW MINUTES. INTENSE RAINS ARE OCCURRING.
COASTAL FLOODING IS AFFECTING ALL MUNICIPALITIES IN EAST AND NORTH-
EAST PUERTO RICO.

AIRBORNE DEBRIS CAN BE OBSERVED AND IS A SERIOUS THREAT. REMAIN
INDOORS.

MEANWHILE IN EASTERN PUERTO RICO...WHERE THE EYE MADE LANDFALL...
THE BACK EDGE OF THE EYE IS REACHING THE COAST. THIS MEANS THE
WINDS ARE BACK AT EXTREME HURRICANE STRENGTH OUT OF THE OPPOSITE
DIRECTION.

REPORTS OUT OF CULEBRA ISLAND INDICATE UP TO 80 PERCENT OF THE
HOMES WERE SEVERELY AFFECTED BY THE FURY OF THE HURRICANE. SIMILAR
REPORTS CAN BE EXPECTED FROM THE NORTHEAST MUNICIPALITIES OF NAGUABO
THROUGH LUQUILLO WHERE THE EYE MADE LANDFALL. NOTHING FURTHER HAS
BEEN HEARD FROM VIEQUES SINCE THEY BECAME INCOMMUNICATED EARLY THIS
MORNING.

THE MOTION OF THE CENTER OF HUGO CONTINUES TO BE IN A GENERAL WEST
NORTHWEST DIRECTION. HOWEVER...HURRICANE EYES TEND TO WOBBLE AS THEY
MOVE...AND THERE IS STILL A POSSIBILITY HUGO'S SWATH OF DESTRUCTION
CONTINUING TO SKIRT ALONG MOST OF THE NORTHERN MUNICIPALITIES OF
PUERTO RICO. OTHER DAMAGING EFFECTS OF THE HURRICANE MAY STILL BE
FELT IN ALL OF PUERTO RICO...THEREFORE NO ONE SHOULD VENTURE OUTSIDE.

TOOHEY/MOJICA
```

Here is an example of how the local weather forecast is issued when the area is under a hurricane warning. Warnings and watches are headlined at the beginning of the forecast text.

```
NY16-SUFFOLK COUNTY EAST OF RIVERHEAD
NY17-TWIN FORKS OF LONG ISLAND
1000 AM EDT FRI SEP 27 1985

...HURRICANE WARNING IN EFFECT...
...FLOOD WATCH IN EFFECT...
...TORNADO WATCH IN EFFECT...

.TODAY...SEVERE WINDS AND HEAVY RAIN CAUSING EXTENSIVE FLOODING IN
MOST AREAS THIS MORNING INTO EARLY THIS AFTERNOON ALONG WITH SOME
THUNDERSTORMS AND POSSIBLY A TORNADO. EXTREMELY HIGH TIDES WILL CAUSE
MAJOR FLOODING ALONG COASTAL SECTIONS ALONG WITH SIGNIFICANT BEACH
EROSION. EASTERLY WINDS 60 TO 80 MPH GUSTING TO OVER 100 MPH THEN
SHIFTING TO THE NORTHWEST BY MID AFTERNOON AND SLOWLY DROPPING OFF.
HIGHS IN THE 70S.

.TONIGHT...CLEARING AND COOLER. LOW 55 TO 60. WINDS NORTHWEST 20 TO
30 MPH AND GUSTY DECREASING GRADUALLY.

.SATURDAY...SUNNY AND BREEZY. HIGH AROUND 70

$$
OUTLOOK FOR SUNDAY..SUNNY AND PLEASANT

A HURRICANE WARNING IS IN EFFECT FOR LONG ISLAND WATERS ALONG WITH A
TORNADO WATCH FOR CENTRAL AND EASTERN SECTIONS.

EDDIE KOCH
```

The National Hurricane Center also issues other products, including strike probabilities, and tropical weather summaries for the climatological historical record.

The NWS also issues a TROPICAL WEATHER DISCUSSION which describes weather features over the North Atlantic from 32°N latitude to the equator, including the Caribbean Sea and Gulf of Mexico, as shown on weather satellite imagery. Below is an example.

```
AXNT20 KNHC 121223
TWDAT
TROPICAL WEATHER DISCUSSION
NATIONAL WEATHER SERVICE MIAMI FL
805 AM EDT THU 12 OCT 1995

THE ATLANTIC OCEAN FROM 32N TO THE EQUATOR...
THE CARIBBEAN SEA...AND THE GULF OF MEXICO.

SPECIAL FEATURE...
..THE CENTER OF HURRICANE ROXANNE IS NEAR 19.4N 91.4W
  AT 12/0900 UTC...MOVING WESTWARD ABOUT 3 KNOTS.
  THE MAXIMUM SUSTAINED WIND SPEED IS 65 KNOTS WITH GUSTS
  TO 80 KNOTS.  SEE THE LATEST NHC ADVISORY UNDER
  AFOS/WMO HEADERS MIATCMAT4/WTNT24 KNHC FOR MORE DETAILS.

SURFACE SYNOPTIC ANALYSIS 12/0600 UTC...
..A CENTRAL ATLANTIC COLD FRONT IS ALONG THE LINE THROUGH
  32N34W-29N50W...CONTINUING AS A STATIONARY FRONT TO
  34N70W...AND INTO THE CENTRAL FLORIDA PENINSULA.  THE
  COLD FRONT IS MOVING EAST-SOUTHEASTWARD AT 5-10 KNOTS.
..AN EASTERN ATLANTIC 1018 MB HIGH CENTER IS NEAR 31N20W.
  HIGH PRESSURE COVERS THE ATLANTIC TO THE NORTH OF 22N
  TO THE EAST OF 30W.
..AN ATLANTIC 1020 MB HIGH CENTER IS NEAR 29N65W.  HIGH
  PRESSURE COVERS THE ATLANTIC WATERS TO THE NORTH OF
  25N BETWEEN 62W AND 73W.
..A TROPICAL WAVE...ASSOCIATED WITH THE REMNANTS OF
  T.S. PABLO...PREVIOUSLY ALONG ALONG 74W/75W...NOW IS
  ALONG 75W/76W...TO THE SOUTH OF 20N...MOVING WESTWARD
  ABOUT 10 KNOTS.
..A TROPICAL WAVE PREVIOUSLY ALONG 49W/50W NOW IS ALONG 51W...
  TO THE SOUTH OF 15N...MOVING WESTWARD AT 10-15 KNOTS.
..A TROPICAL WAVE PREVIOUSLY ALONG 25W/26W...NOW IS ALONG 27W...
  TO THE SOUTH OF 15N...MOVING WESTWARD AT 10-15 KNOTS.

INTERPRETATION OF SATELLITE IMAGERY THROUGH 12/1045 UTC...

HURRICANE ROXANNE...
SCATTERED STRONG CONVECTION IS INDICATED OVER INTERIOR
SECTIONS OF THE YUCATAN PENINSULA AND SOUTHEASTERN MEXICO...
GUATEMALA...BELIZE...AND THE GULF OF HONDURAS FROM 15.5N
TO 18.5N BETWEEN 86W AND 92W.

GULF OF MEXICO...MESOSCALE FEATURES...
BROKEN TO OVERCAST MULTILAYERED CLOUDS COVER THE GULF WATERS
TO THE WEST OF 90W.  SCATTERED MODERATE TO ISOLATED STRONG
CONVECTION IS FOUND IN CLUSTERS FROM 27N TO 28N BETWEEN 92W
AND 94W...FROM 23N TO 25N BETWEEN 94W AND 96W...BECOMING
ISOLATED OVER THE REST OF THE GULF TO THE SOUTH OF 25N
TO THE WEST OF 90W.

CARIBBEAN SEA...
NUMEROUS STRONG THUNDERSTORMS ARE OCCURRING FROM THE COASTS
OF VENEZUELA AND COLOMBIA TO 13N BETWEEN 70W AND 75W...AS WELL
AS FROM 14N TO 18N BETWEEN 72W AND 74W.  SCATTERED MODERATE
TO ISOLATED STRONG CONVECTION IS LOCATED FROM 10N TO 13N
BETWEEN 76W AND 80W...FROM 12N TO 20N BETWEEN 80W AND 83W...
AND TO THE NORTH OF 17N BETWEEN 75W AND 80W.

SUBTROPICAL ATLANTIC...
SCATTERED SHOWERS AND MODERATE THUNDERSTORMS ARE FOUND OVER
THE WATERS FROM 10N TO 12N BETWEEN 46W AND 50W...AND TO THE
NORTH OF 30N BETWEEN 28W AND 32W.

TROPICAL ATLANTIC...
SCATTERED MODERATE TO ISOLATED STRONG CONVECTION IS INDICATED
WITHIN 180 NM OF THE AFRICAN COAST FROM LIBERIA TO SIERRA LEONE
TO GUINEA...AS WELL AS FROM 11N TO 16N BETWEEN 19W AND 23W.
SCATTERED MODERATE TO ISOLATED STRONG CONVECTION IS WITHIN
120 NM ON EITHER SIDE OF THE LINE 9N24W-7N30W...AND WITHIN
150 NM ON EITHER SIDE OF 6N BETWEEN 33W AND 43W.  SCATTERED
MODERATE CONVECTION IS SEEN FROM 7N TO 12N BETWEEN 47W AND 54W.

TICHACEK
```

Figure 113. A cutaway depiction of a hurricane. The vertical view is exaggerated to show detail. Actual cloud tops of most tropical cyclones are about 50,000 feet. The horizontal extent of most hurricanes is several hundred miles. (source: NOAA)